WILDFLOWERS 1

THE CASCADES ▪ BY ELIZABETH L. HORN

Introduction by
KENTON L. CHAMBERS, PH.D.
Professor of Botany
Oregon State University

all my love to the most beautiful flower of them all — who is only slightly wild,

Jim.

THE TOUCHSTONE PRESS
P. O. Box 81
Beaverton, Oregon 97005

LIBRARY OF CONGRESS
Catalog Card Number 78-189511

INTRODUCTION

Preparing a handbook about the wildflowers of a region such as the Cascade Mountains is in some respects easier than discussing, for example, the birds, mammals, or reptiles of the same area. Plants are immobile, passive (if you discount the thorny blackberries, stinging nettles, and irritating poison-oak), and are faithful to their particular habitats and life zones. A beautiful meadow of alpine flowers can be visited year after year, with assurance that the same familiar species of flowers will reappear, as though on cue, throughout the season. The ease with which plants can be studied and photographed is in contrast to the difficulties presented by the elusive and highly mobile animals that occupy these same habitats. Compared with a zoologist, therefore, the botanical writer's job is simpler because he can assume his audience will very likely be able to find the flowers he is describing and will be able to study them leisurely and in detail.

It should not be assumed, however, that plant study is in all respects easier or less challenging than the study of animals. The difficulty one has with wildflowers, in a word, is that there are so many different varieties. If we include with the wildflowers all the trees, shrubs, grass-like plants and ferns, there probably could be listed close to 1000 species for the middle to high elevations of the Cascade Mountains, between northern California and southern Washington. This is merely an educated guess, because no complete list is available. Counts have been made for limited areas, and in Crater Lake National Park, for example, there are 550 species. The author of an introductory handbook of wildflowers must therefore be selective, and must narrow down the choice of possible species to a workable list. A user of the book is in this way guided to the most common and conspicuous members of the flora. Once having mastered these, he still may look forward to the pleasure of familiarizing himself with the variety of other types—the less showy plants and the rare novelties—that are discussed only in more specialized botanical works.

In Beth Horn's book there are more than 180 kinds of wildflowers described, the majority illustrated with color photographs and the approach to identification is simple and direct. The reader first notes the general habitat in which the plant is growing, and then with the assistance of its flower color and other characteristics, matches the plant with its appropriate illustration and description. There is an added advantage to this emphasis on the habitats and environments which plants occupy, because it sharpens one's awareness of the repeating patterns formed by natural vegetation. It is these natural patterns, expressed as a series of relatively stable plant communities, which are so often upset or destroyed by man's careless treatment of nature's handiwork. The reader of this book will be better able to understand the biological concept of "the web of life," after he discovers the regularity with which many plant species occupy only a given environment and no other, and after he notes the ubiquitous weeds which invade and displace the original vegetation in sites that have been disturbed by man's activities.

In addition to being objects of beauty and essential threads in the fabric of vegetational communities, wildflowers may have special importance to man as food plants or medicinal herbs, or even as toxic plants which may cause the death of grazing animals or of humans themselves. Throughout the following pages, Beth Horn has included much information from this practical side of botany, gleaned from books on Indian lore and from standard treatises on medicinal and poisonous plants. While the validity of many so-called folk remedies is open to question on medical grounds, there is nonetheless a continuing interest in natural plant products and their uses, as for example the native plants that can provide "survival food" for outdoorsmen lost in the wilds. Many readers may find information such as this to be of practical value, both in recognizing those species that are edible and in avoiding the ones that are known to be dangerously toxic.

We in the Pacific Northwest, residents and visitors alike, are at a turning point in our relationship with the water, lands, forests, and mountains that constitute our essential natural resources. There is a great need for more knowledge and appreciation of these resources, and in particular of their recreational value for those of us who must escape, now and then, from a hectic urbanized environment. The Cascade Mountains, which were once a forested wilderness crossed only by a few pioneer wagon tracks, are now accessible by road and trail to even the most casual weekend traveler. Although the once magnificent stands of trees have been cut from the lower mountain slopes and are being slowly regenerated, the higher elevation landscape still presents much of the character of an original wild country. In these highlands occur the commanding displays of summer wildflowers, so colorful and diverse, that challenge the skills of an amateur naturalist. Some species, such as bear-grass and rhododendron, may be familiar acquaintances from the distant wooded shores of the Pacific ocean, while others, like mountain heather, are found only in alpine environments. Because this flora has, in so many respects, a uniquely alpine and subalpine character, it forms a conveniently defined unit which can be reduced to the manageable size appropriate for a field guide.

Travelers, hikers, and vacationers in the Cascade Mountains will find this book a useful and interesting introduction to the common, conspicuous plants to be encountered in this scenic area. The carefully chosen illustrations and concise text should permit ready identification of the included species, and should help toward an understanding of the distribution of plants across the range of characteristic montane habitats. Persons who are interested in the potential uses of plants and their edible qualities will appreciate the information which the author has included on these subjects. There has long been a need for a useful and well-illustrated guide to our mountain wildflowers. We are indebted to Beth Horn for providing such a work, which will be a valued companion on many enjoyable hikes through the botanical realms of the Cascades.

Kenton L. Chambers

FOREWORD

Mountains have a particular appeal for most people. We seek their solace for weekends of relaxation, and for extended vacations. Campers, picnickers, back-packers, and fishermen alike appreciate the grand alpine scenery. A splendid element in the high vistas are meadows of colorful wildflowers, which bloom profusely once the snow pack melts from the upper elevations. But, earlier we can find wildflowers everywhere: around campsites in the deep woodlands, aside montane lakes and streams, and along the alpine trails.

Flowers, like people, are much more interesting and appealing if we know their names and a little about them. Is the fruit edible? Does this plant get any bigger? Where else can it be found? In turn, knowing some of the nearby wildflowers helps make you more aware and appreciative of the rest of your surroundings.

This book was written to help you locate and identify some of the more common and conspicuous wildflowers found in the volcanic Cascade Mountains, which extend from central Washington into northern California. This mountain range is dominated by cone-shaped peaks such as Mt. Rainier, Mt. Adams, Mt. Hood, Mt. Jefferson, the Three Sisters, Mt. Shasta, and Lassen Peak. All of the flowering species in such a large geographical area could not be treated in a book of this size. Instead, an attempt was made to choose those plants that would be encountered most often throughout the area—the more typical Cascade species.

Many specific locations are noted where a wildflower may be found. These are not the only locations a particular flower or shrub may occur: a few places are simply given as examples. Most of the plants listed in this book grow throughout the Cascades and you will find them in many other areas similar to those listed.

In some cases, where individual species are hard to distinguish (such as larkspur, goldenrod, wild rose) a flower typical of the group was chosen for discussion. Many of these same flowers can be found throughout the Sierra Nevada and northern Rockies, and some grow in the colder regions of Eurasia as well. In addition to giving the common and scientific names of the plants covered, this book also relates some interesting information on the uses that the Indians and early settlers in the West had for some of our native mountain plants. Botanical terminology has been kept to a minimum. With the help of the color photos and simple descriptions, you should have no trouble identifying the plants covered in this book. An illustrated glossary and bibliography have been provided at the back of the book.

Mountain plants, especially those growing above timberline, are very slow developing. If picked or trampled, it may be a long time before a new plant grows to replace it, because the growing season is short and the climate severe. Careless hikers who cut switchbacks or scramble up steep slopes aid erosion and dislodge plants that may have taken years to grow. Those who have visited the high Cascades over the past ten years tell of once lush meadows now criss-crossed with paths and many areas of bare dirt where flowers once bloomed. PLEASE— leave the mountains as beautiful as you found them. Stay on the established paths, and do not pick or otherwise destroy the flowers of an alpine meadow.

Carry this book with you when you go into the mountains. It can be a helpful companion. It was designed to be packed and used easily. And, don't feel that you must be a rugged individualist to get to the areas of mountain flowers. While it is true that some species grow best only in out-of-the-way places or on high alpine peaks, many others are very much at home along roadsides and in the open meadows next to campgrounds. Some very excellent wildflower "gardens" are along paved roads. The Mt. Hood Meadows and Timberline Lodge areas on Mt. Hood, the Paradise Valley area of Mt. Rainier, and the Castle Crest Wildflower Garden within Crater Lake National Park are just a few excellent examples. There are many more.

Once you learn a few of the flowers in your favorite spot, do not feel that you will have to begin over again in another area of the Cascades. The colorful spreading phlox that you encounter along the Timberline Trail on Mt. Hood will be like an old friend when you find it again on Mt. Rainier or along the rim of Crater Lake. You will find this to be true of many of the plants listed in this book, so take it with you to Lassen Peak and the Goat Rocks and see how many old friends you will find!

Government Camp, Oregon   E.L.H.
January, 1972

CONTENTS

Introduction   Page 3

Foreword   Page 6

How to Use This Book   Page 8

The Vegetation of the Cascade Mountains   Page 9

Alpine Adaptations   Page 14

About Scientific Names   Page 15

Acknowledgments   Page 16

Section I—Coniferous Forests, Deeply Shaded Woodlands   Page 17

Section II—Dry Openings in Coniferous Forests   Page 55

Section III—Moist Areas Below Timberline   Page 91

Section IV—Timberline and Alpine Areas   Page 120

Glossary   Page 152

Index   Page 155

For Further Reading   Page 158

Flower Photo Tips   Page 159

HOW TO USE THIS BOOK

There are more than 180 plant descriptions in this book, illustrated by 140 color photographs. When you find an alpine wildflower that you do not know, you could simply start paging through the book, hoping to find a photo that resembles the flower in question. However, to save time, you might first take a look around you. Where is the flower? Is it above timberline? By a stream? In a wet meadow? By a lakeshore? On a rocky slope? Under the deep shade of a mountain hemlock? Take a good look at where it is growing—its habitat.

This book is divided into four sections, each covering a typical alpine or subalpine habitat.

Section One: deep, shaded or open conifer woods, areas where there is little sunlight penetrating to the floor of the forest. The Cascades are known for lush forests of Douglas fir, western hemlock, mountain hemlock, silver fir, and red fir, in addition to the drier, more open woodlands of lodgepole and ponderosa pine. Many flowers grow in the shade of these forests, especially members of the orchid and heath families.

Section Two: dry forest openings, including areas along roadsides, or woodland borders, on sunny rocky outcrops, and in dry grassy meadows. Many sun-loving plants thrive in these well-drained open sites; for instance, look for the stronecrops and penstemons.

Section Three: wet areas below timberline. Stream and lake borders, wet meadows, marshes, and bogs are inhabited by a wide variety of mountain plants.

Section Four: timberline and above. This section includes the flowers found in the open, park-like meadows near timberline, where small clumps of trees punctuate the open areas. This is where you will find the most vivid wildflower displays.

Most plants are found typically in one type of area. The four sections of this book correspond to the usual habitats for Cascade wildflowers and should help you find the plant in question in a minimum amount of time. The flowers within each section are arranged by family so that similar flowers are together and thus easy to compare. However, if you see the plant in more than one type of habitat, choose the area where it seems most typical—although you found it along a forest border, it might thrive in open woodlands, too. A dry, rocky area at a moderate elevation may simulate conditions above timberline, so look first in Section Two, then in Section Four.

Comparison of the plant with the photograph and the printed description should make identification fairly easy. And, to make your hike or auto trip even more interesting, try studying the book first, then take it with you to see how many of the flowers displayed here you can find in their natural habitat.

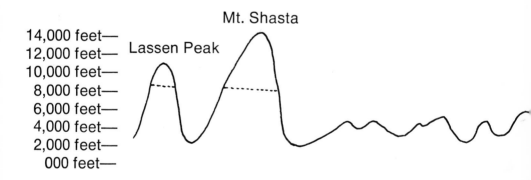

Mt. Shasta

14,000 feet—
12,000 feet—   Lassen Peak
10,000 feet—
8,000 feet—
6,000 feet—
4,000 feet—
2,000 feet—
000 feet—

THE VEGETATION OF THE CASCADE MOUNTAINS

Biologists in the western states have long recognized similar collections of various species or communities of plants from one mountainous area to the next, closely related to those found farther north. For instance, the vegetation found around timberline in the Northwest is similar in many ways to that found in the circumpolar areas of North America, the far northern areas referred to as the Arctic tundra. Mountains in the western United States have similar areas where the vegetation consists mainly of low, mat-forming plants. Many alpine plants circle the world's arctic regions and also extend southward along high mountain chains.

Below timberline is a belt of coniferous (evergreen) forests closely resembling those found across the northern regions of North America. These coniferous forests are found also in the Cascades. Biologists have drawn hypothetical mountains with zones appearing as sequential belts around them, each zone being characterized by representative plants and animals. However, such a diagram oversimplifies the situation, since small variations in topography and the presence of ridges and valleys will greatly change the location of a zone.

Plant ecologists—those who study the relationship of plants to their surroundings—generally use a system of zonation based on the plants found in each area. The presence or absence of these plant species reflects the local topography, climate, and exposure. Generally speaking, the elevation of each zone varies with its northern latitude. Therefore, a rise in elevation of about 1000 feet is equal to a latitudinal move 300 miles to the north. Thus, a given vegetation zone on the south slopes of Lassen Peak occurs at a higher elevation than the corresponding zone on Mt. Hood. The accompanying diagram illustrates this point.

The lowland forests of the Cascade Mountains form the major timber-producing region of the Northwest. On the western slopes of northern and central Oregon and Washington western hemlock *(Tsuga heterophylla)* and Douglas fir *(Pseudotsuga menziesii)* are the most conspicuous trees, with white fir *(Abies concolor)* replacing western hemlock south of the Umpqua Divide in southern Oregon. In places disturbed by fire, logging, or both, almost pure stands of Douglas fir may occur. Ponderosa (or yellow) pine *(Pinus ponderosa)* is found on the eastern slopes and forms a drier, more open forest. In places it is interspersed with stands of lodgepole pine and may have manzanita growing beneath. (Lodgepole pine may also be found on the western slopes of the Cascades, at higher elevations, especially when an area has been burned.)

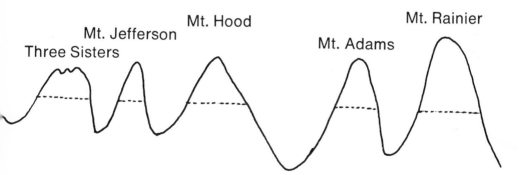

Approximately 600 miles separate Lassen Peak from Mt. Rainier.
Mountain zones are lower as one moves north—timberline on
Lassen Peak lies above 9,000 feet; on Mt. Rainier it lies above 6,000 feet.

An almost continuous mantle of forest covers the upper reaches of the Cascades, up to timberline. It is sometimes referred to as the Subalpine Forest. Silver fir *(Abies amabilis)* and Shasta red fir *(Abies magnifica* var *shastensis)* are the main trees in the lower portions of this zone, silver fir being replaced by Shasta red fir south of McKenzie Pass. A great variety of smaller plants may be found growing below these firs. It is here that one would most likely encounter the beautifully-flowered Pacific rhododendron, huckleberry, pyrola, bunchberry, twinflower, and queen's cup, all species requiring cool, moist, shaded woodlands.

Mountain hemlock *(Tsuga mertensiana)* is the main species found in the upper part of the Subalpine Forest, being found along the crest of the Cascades just below timberline. Mountain hemlock typically forms a very dense forest, and little sun penetrates to the ground. However, near timberline, there are numerous small meadows and openings. The subalpine fir *(Abies lasiocarpa)*, with its symmetrical, conical shape, grows amid the hemlock and borders many of the meadows at timberline.

Throughout the Subalpine Forest there are many openings: dry meadows, bogs, marshes, lakes, forest clear-cuts, lava fields, and rocky slopes. Plants such as the bog orchid, camas, and grass-of-parnassus may be found in the wetter areas while penstemon, beargrass, fireweed and stonecrop inhabit the drier spots.

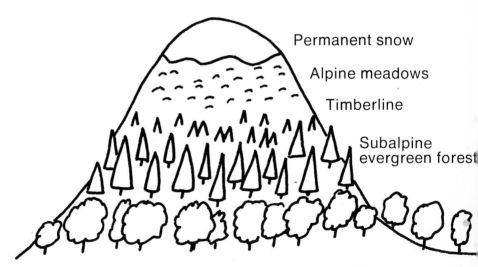

Permanent snow

Alpine meadows

Timberline

Subalpine
evergreen forest

Lowland forest

Timberline is found only on the highest peaks, such as Mt. Hood, Mt. Jefferson, Mt. Rainier, the Three Sisters, Shasta, Lassen Peak and other scattered areas. Often referred to as the Alpine Zone, it is a mosaic of small clumps of trees and open, grassy meadows at timberline and rocky scree above timberline. Various definitions of timberline have been used by different authors. It may be the upper limit of upright trees, the upper limit of continuous trees, or the upper limit of krummholz (wind-pruned timber), often called the scrub line. (In this book, timberline is the upper limit of continuous trees.) The most common timberline trees are the subalpine fir, mountain hemlock, and whitebark pine *(Pinus albicaulis)*. All of these may be picturesque, wind-trained trees or may become reduced to low-growing, matted shrubs. There are many grassy meadows and "rock gardens" that may blaze with color during the short alpine summer. The various species of heather, vivid displays of paintbrush, mats of partridge-foot, dwarf lupine, anemone, cinquefoil, and aster are a few of the plants that may be found above timberline.

The various forest types found on the Cascade Mountains have assured a variety of plant species growing beneath them. Each area has slightly different climatic conditions of temperature and moisture, which are, in turn, influenced by local topography produced by ridges and valleys. You can observe this variety for yourself when you travel through the Cascade Mountains of the Northwest.

N→

Evergreen forests of
North America

Polar
Ice cap

Arctic
tundra

Temperate forests of
North America

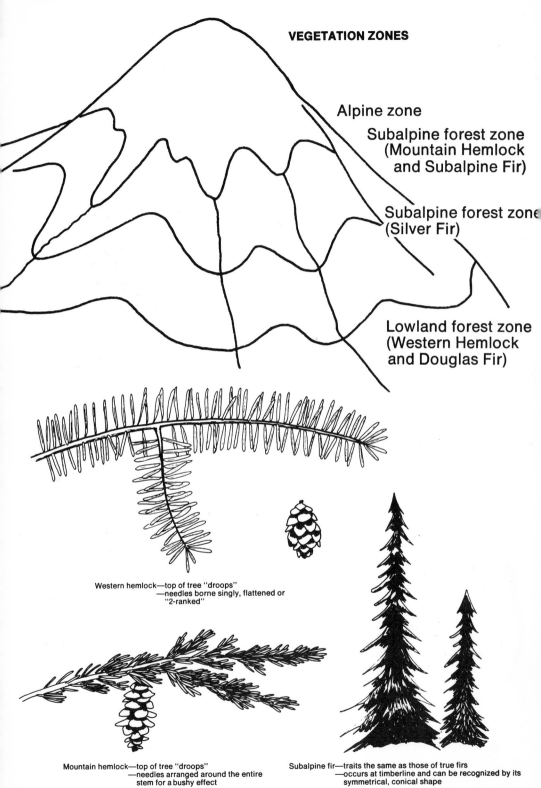

VEGETATION ZONES

Alpine zone

Subalpine forest zone
(Mountain Hemlock
and Subalpine Fir)

Subalpine forest zone
(Silver Fir)

Lowland forest zone
(Western Hemlock
and Douglas Fir)

Western hemlock—top of tree "droops"
—needles borne singly, flattened or
"2-ranked"

Mountain hemlock—top of tree "droops"
—needles arranged around the entire
stem for a bushy effect

Subalpine fir—traits the same as those of true firs
—occurs at timberline and can be recognized by its
symmetrical, conical shape

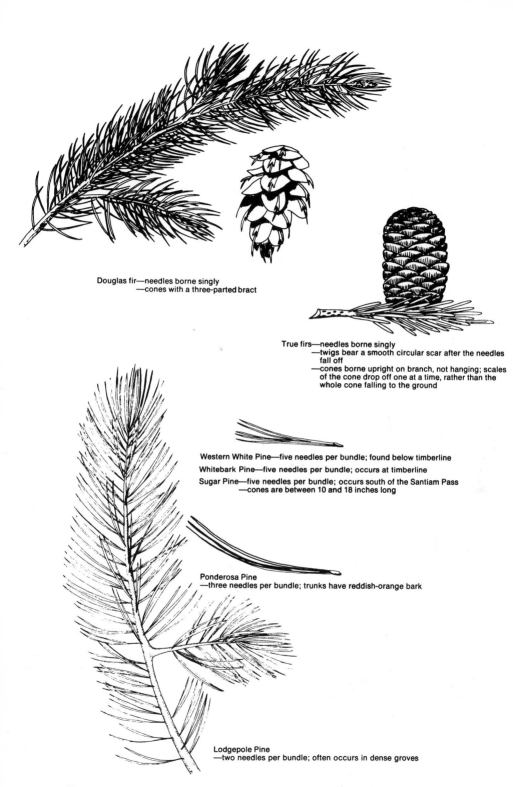

Douglas fir—needles borne singly
—cones with a three-parted bract

True firs—needles borne singly
—twigs bear a smooth circular scar after the needles fall off
—cones borne upright on branch, not hanging; scales of the cone drop off one at a time, rather than the whole cone falling to the ground

Western White Pine—five needles per bundle; found below timberline

Whitebark Pine—five needles per bundle; occurs at timberline

Sugar Pine—five needles per bundle; occurs south of the Santiam Pass
—cones are between 10 and 18 inches long

Ponderosa Pine
—three needles per bundle; trunks have reddish-orange bark

Lodgepole Pine
—two needles per bundle; often occurs in dense groves

Pines—needles borne in clusters, with a thin sheath at the base of each cluster

ALPINE ADAPTATIONS

The climate near timberline is characterized by short, cool growing seasons and long, snowy winters. In fact, snow flurries may come at any time during the year. Patches of snow last well into the summer, even below timberline.

Several factors discourage plant growth at these elevations. The short growing season alone hampers the formation of lush vegetation, for there simply is not enough time for plants to attain extensive vegetative growth before the fall snows begin. Soil development is slow, there being little or no vegetative cover to break down the bedrock or form humus. So the soil remains rocky and porous, unable to store water, a factor that again limits plant growth. In addition, alternate freezing and thawing makes the soil unstable. Even after a plant has begun to grow, a rock slide may uproot it.

Wind velocity increases with elevation and strong, constant winds intensify the problems of soil development and adverse climate. Plants at high elevations must not only be able to absorb and store water when it is available, but must then avoid desiccation from the evaporative winds.

Cold, unstable soil, wind and lack of water combine to create a brutal environment. Alpine plants have developed both physiological and morphological means of adapting to their surroundings. A few of the latter are listed below.

GROWTH SHAPE—Many alpine plants are extremely small—they grow slowly, perhaps only inches a year, storing up manufactured food in their roots and stems. The low, matted form helps avoid the drying winds, since the friction caused by the earth itself tends to slow wind close to the ground. Cracks, crevices, and hollows also provide a low-growing plant protection. The compact, ball-like form reduces the effect of the wind and cold. The wind is dissipated within a grove of trees. Such is the case also with a spreading phlox, small lupine, or other ground-hugging plants that grow in dense mats. Outer leaves protect the inner growth. This dense foliage becomes a heat trap, too, absorbing the sun's warmth much more efficiently than could a single-stalked plant. The added heat helps speed the plant's growth.

PERENNIAL FORM—Many plants avoid cold simply by being dormant most of the year. Very few mountain plants are annuals (plants living only one year, depending on seeds to re-establish them the next year). The growing season is not long enough to allow seeds to sprout, and the plant to grow, produce flowers, and bear seeds. Most alpine plants become dormant during the winter, sometimes waiting several seasons to produce flowers. These plants are called perennials.

ROOTS—Since very little moisture is available in mountain soil once the snow melt-water has been used up, plants produce extensive root systems. The longer the roots, the better is the chance of encountering water. They also serve as storage organs. *Polygonum newberryi* is only about 6 inches tall. But it has tubers extending two feet below the ground, and small roots reaching even farther. By the end of the summer, the stems dry up and blow away. Protected underground, the roots remain and contain enough stored food to send up new shoots the following spring. Large roots, in addition, help secure a plant on a slope of loose rock, where winds and rolling stones would dislodge a shallow-rooted plant.

LEAVES—A great deal of water is lost from leaf surfaces. When roots have an adequate supply of water, this is no problem. But in the alpine region a plant must curtail its water loss if it is to survive. Most leaves are very small, reducing the surface-to-volume ratio. Many leaves are thick and have waxy coverings to reduce evaporation from their surfaces. Others have fuzzy or hairy coverings, which retard evaporation and cut the force of the drying winds. Evergreen leaves can also be valuable to a plant. Not only do they generally have thick cuticles covering them, but are also an advantage for a short growing season. It is much more economical to use a set of leaves for more than one season.

ABOUT SCIENTIFIC NAMES

Even the beginning botanist should attempt to learn some scientific names. Common names may be very confusing. For instance, the beargrass found on Mt. Hood and Mt. Rainier is not the same beargrass as that found in the mesas and mountains of the Southwest. The flower commonly called dogtooth violet is not really a violet at all, but a member of the lily family. To add to the confusion, some plants have more than one common name. The names shadblow, serviceberry, mountain pear, and Juneberry are only a few of the names applied to one shrub common throughout the Cascades. Another shrub goes by the names of ocean spray, creambush, and arrow-wood. There are many such examples. Usually these names originate from different localities: people living in one area call a plant by one name, while others use a different name. A scientific name, however, can only be used for one plant. *Pyrola secunda*—commonly called shin-leaf or one-sided pyrola—is *Pyrola secunda* whether encountered in Oregon, Arizona, or Europe.

All plants fall under fairly natural groupings or families. The members of each family look somewhat alike and have many floral chacteristics that are similar. The family of each plant discussed in this book is listed at the beginning of each plant description. Every family is composed of several genera. Each genus, in turn, is divided into one or more species. This is the individual plant.

Let us look at the paintbrush, a common plant of the Cascade Range, to see how this works. It belongs to the Figwort family of plants, the genus *Castilleja*. The paintbrush is just one type of figwort, however. There are many more, a few of which are shown in this diagram:

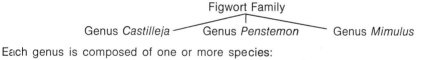

Figwort Family

Genus *Castilleja*   Genus *Penstemon*   Genus *Mimulus*

Each genus is composed of one or more species:

Castilleja

hispida   miniata   parviflora

Every plant has two words making up its scientific name; *Castilleja hispida* is our example. *Castilleja* is the genus or generic name and hispida is the species or specific name for a particular type of paintbrush.

The scientific name is usually derived from Greek or Latin words. The genus name is a noun and often is indicative of some characteristic of that particular group of plants. For instance, the genus name *Corallorhiza* is used for a group of orchids with roots resembling pieces of coral. Sometimes the genus name honors a person—*Castilleja* is derived from the name of a Spanish botanist. The species name is usually a descriptive term. Such words as hispida (meaning hairy), triphylla (three leaves), ovalifolium (oval or round leaf) and secunda (one-sided) are good examples. The specific name may also honor a person. The scientific name of the Pacific dogwood, *Cornus nuttallii,* illustrates these points. *Cornus* comes from the Greek word for horn and refers to the hardness of the wood. The specific name honors the man who first discovered the tree as a new species, Thomas Nuttall. Sometimes it is impossible to know the real meaning of some scientific names, especially when the name is extremely old. However, in cases where the meanings are fairly well-established, they are incorporated into the plant descriptions contained in this book.

ACKNOWLEDGMENTS

As is the case with most tasks, this book is not solely the work of the author. Many others have been helpful and encouraging along the way, and without them this book would have been much less enjoyable and more difficult to produce. The staff of the Oregon State University Herbarium, notably Dr. LaRea Dennis Johnston and Dr. Kenton Chambers helped with the identification of numerous flower specimens, and I appreciated their cheerfully given assistance. In addition, Dr. Chambers made many suggestions that have been incorporated into the book. Dr. Alton A. Lindsey, plant ecologist at Purdue University, read the manuscript also, and his critique made it more accurate and readable. Dr. Jerry Franklin, plant ecologist with the Forest and Range Experiment Station, U.S. Forest Service, Portland, Oregon, read the section on mountain zonation and helped with information on the ecology of several of the plants treated here. Any mistakes left in this volume are in spite of these people and are solely my doings!

Lastly, I wish to acknowledge the one who gave me the idea—Kirk Horn. He assisted in many other ways, too. He helped proofread and select photos—and took the pictures appearing on the cover and pages 5 and 121. Perhaps most important, he was always patient when I chased after various plants during our many hikes in the high Cascades.

Elizabeth L. Horn

WOOD TRILLIUM
Trillium ovatum
LILY Family

Also called wake-robin. Growing under partial shade in damp wooded areas, the trillium is a forerunner of springtime, blooming as early as March along the coast through late June at higher elevations in the mountains. The plant stands 6 to 24 inches tall and has but one flower composed of three white petals, elevated from three ovate leaves by a short stalk. The petals darken with age, slowly becoming pink. *Range:* British Columbia south through Oregon to central California, east to the northern Rocky Mountains.

Wood Trillium

QUEEN'S CUP
Clintonia uniflora
LILY Family

Also called bead-lily. Only two or three oblong basal leaves support this plant's single white flower, which is elevated about 4 inches on its floral stalk. The solitary flower is followed by a round, blue berry. The horizontal stems grow just under the ground, allowing the plant to spread and cover a large area. Look for it in the partial shade of the forest where it blooms from May through July. This is a mountain-loving species, found in the Cascade forests of Oregon, Washington, and northern California.

Range: Mountains of southern Alaska south to the central Sierra Nevada, east to the mountains of Montana.

TIGER LILY
Lilium columbianum
LILY Family

This tall lily graces roadsides and forest openings from the lowlands to moderate elevations in the mountains. The stem may be from 1 to 6 feet tall (about 3 feet is the common height), and has from one to several orange blossoms, which are spotted with flecks of brown, yellow, or dark purple. There is a great deal of variation in the shape and arrangement of the leaves and flowers, and, since it is easily cultivated, it adorns many gardens. As is true of all the lilies, the root is a large bulb. Being edible, it was used as food by the Pacific Northwest Indians.

Range: British Columbia south in the Cascades to the Sierra Nevada, east to Idaho and Nevada.

Tiger Lily

FALSE SOLOMON'S SEAL
Smilacina racemosa
LILY Family

Growing from an underground rootstalk, the false Solomon's seal is characterized by a single, unbranched stem (10 to 30 inches long) with a plume of small white flowers. It is abundant in moist woods from April through June, depending on elevation. Its red berries are edible. Often growing with it is the star-flowered Solomon's seal *(S. stellata),* distinguished by more sharply pointed leaves and fewer, star-shaped flowers. Its stem is 1 or 2 feet long. Also growing from an underground rootstock, star-flowered Solomon's seal may appear to be growing in a small colony. The Indians used the root of this species in healing wounds.

Range: Widespread throughout the United States.

Star-flowered Solomon's Seal

False Solomon's Seal

WILD LILY-OF-THE-VALLEY
Maianthemum dilatata
LILY Family

Deep in the shade of the Northwest's luxuriant forests, this small lily might escape attention. However, its leaves alone attract notice. A short, 3 to 12 inch stem carries one or two shiny, heart-shaped leaves. These cover large areas of the forest floor, creating an unbroken carpet. In the spring and summer each plant bears a stalk of tiny, white flowers and their faint odor scents the air. These are followed by edible, bright red berries, once used as food by the Indians. Wild lily-of-the-valley grows beneath the Douglas fir and hemlock forests of moderate elevations.

Range: Alaska south, mainly along the coast and in the Cascades, to central California, east to Idaho and central British Columbia.

TWAYBLADE
Listera caurina
ORCHID Family

The orchids comprise one of the largest plant families in the world. There are about 8,000 species of orchids known, although some authorities feel there may be more than 30,000 members of this group. Orchids reach their greatest development in the tropics, but many can also be found in more temperate climates. Orchids living in cooler areas usually grow in damp situations: mountain meadows or bogs or the floor of moist, shaded forests. Some woodland orchids are saprophytic—they derive their nourishment from the decaying material of dead plants. Orchids are among the most striking and complex flowers known. Two of their three petals are alike, the third being tubular, bulbous, spurred, flat, or otherwise variously shaped. It is this third petal that contributes most to the odd and conspicuous shape of the flower and is called the lip.

The twayblade is a shade-loving plant, between 4 and 12 inches tall. The unbranched stem has two broad, sessile leaves and small, incon-spicuous greenish flowers borne at the tip. Easily over-looked because it blends into the surrounding undergrowth, it grows on the floor of moist conifer forests and along stream-banks, from moderate elevations to subalpine slopes.

Another twayblade *L. cordata,* often grows alongside. It is shorter, its stems being between 3 and 8 inches tall. The lower lip of this flower has a deep notch in it while the lip of *L. caurina* is whole. There are probably 20 species of *Listera* in the cooler regions of the northern hemisphere.

Range: Southern Alaska and British Columbia south through Oregon to northern California, east to Idaho and Montana.

Twayblade

PURPLE CORAL-ROOT
Corallorhiza mertensiana
ORCHID Family

Coral-roots derive all their nourishment from decaying plants, producing none of their own as do plants with green leaves and stems. Coral-root stems are brown, yellow, or purple in color, and the leaves have degenerated into scales along the stem. Coral-root flowers have one petal that forms a broad, expanded lip. The underground stem is divided into short, knobby sections, resembling a piece of coral and is responsible for the name. The Greek word *korallion* (meaning coral) and *riza* (meaning root) form the basis for the generic name.

There are about 15 species of coral-root in temperate North America.

Purple coral-root grows 8 to 20 inches tall and is common in the moist coniferous forests of the Cascades at moderate elevations. Its flowers have a spurred lip and are a purplish or reddish color. The lip itself, is plain, being the same color as the rest of the flower.

The striped coral-root *(C. striata)* also occurs in similar situations. It lacks the floral spur present in the purple coral-root, and its lip is striped with brown or purple. Still another coral-root *(C. maculata)* may be found in damp coniferous forests, being more common in Lassen Volcanic National Park and the California mountains. Like the purple coral-root, it has a spurred lip; however, in this case the lip is decorated with purple spots, giving rise to its common name, spotted coral-root.

Range: Alaska south to northern California, east to western Montana and Wyoming.

26

VENUS SLIPPER
Calypso bulbosa
ORCHID Family

Also called calypso, fairy-slipper, angel slipper. The dainty, slipper-shaped purple flowers of this species need little introduction to most natives of the Northwest. From 4 to 7 inches tall, this plant grows in the leaf mold of deep, moist coniferous woods from sea level to middle elevations in the mountains. It is common on the lower reaches of Mt. Hood, and other woodland areas on the slopes of the Cascades.

The genus was named for the Greek sea nymph Kalypso, of Homer's Odyssey, the word meaning covered or hidden. And it is well that this flower usually grows hidden beneath other shrubs and ferns, for in many areas it has been picked so often that it is now rare. When orchids are picked, fewer seeds are produced, and the chance for new plants to be established is lessened.

Orchids have become so specialized that they often must rely on a single type of insect to pollinate them, and even when seeds are produced, they will not germinate unless certain fungi are present. The root system of *Calypso* is not extensive. Alone it probably could not support the plant. However, the roots of all orchids are closely associated with mycorhizae (fungi filaments). The *Calypso* mycorhizae transfer nutrients from the decaying material in the soil to the orchid.

Range: Widespread across northern North America and in the mountains of the western states.

Venus Slipper

RATTLESNAKE ORCHID
Goodyera oblongifolia
ORCHID Family

The deep green, leathery leaves, growing in a low rosette and each with distinctive white vein-markings, quickly identify the rattlesnake orchid. These leaves are evergreen, so may be seen at any time of the year the ground is free of snow. About one foot tall, the flower stalk bears small white waxy flowers, growing compactly along the upper portion. Found mainly in dense conifer forests, it often forms small colonies.

Range: Widespread across northern North America and in the western United States.

Rattlesnake Orchid

WILD GINGER
Asarum caudatum
BIRTHWORT Family

The sprawling rootstocks of this plant grow freely through the leaf mold of damp woods, with pairs of long-petioled (2 to 8 inches long) heart-shaped leaves emerging at the tips. The leaves are deep green above and light green below, covered with soft, woolly hairs that give the leaves a velvety texture. The dark rose-colored flowers, hidden beneath these leaves, can be hard to find amid the dead leaves and twigs on the forest floor.

The roots, stems, and leaves all emit an aromatic, ginger-like fragrance. Although the ginger of commerce belongs to an entirely different family of plants and grows mainly in the tropics, the roots of the eastern *Asarum,* also called wild ginger, were widely gathered by the early settlers as a ginger substitute. The women dried and grated them, using the flakes as a spice. There are twenty or more species of wild ginger in North America and Eurasia, six of which are found in the United States.

Range: British Columbia south to central California, east to western Montana.

29

Wild Ginger

CANDYFLOWER
Montia sibirica
PURSLANE Family

The small, white blossoms of candyflower are quite showy. They have five notched petals, which may have faint pink streaks on them. The ovate or spatulate basal leaves may form a tangle completely covering the ground. However, the 5 to 12 inch long stem bears only two oval leaves, opposite each other. These leaves are sessile—meaning they do not have a stalk (or petiole), but are attached directly to the stem of the plant. Look for candyflower in moist, shady areas, especially along tree-lined streams, throughout the summer. The whole plant is very tender and may be used for salad greens.

Although the species name indicates that candyflower was first thought to have been discovered in Siberia, or at least to grow there, it is doubtful that it really occurs there. It does, however, grow in the islands off Alaska.

Range: Alaska south through southern California, east to Montana and Utah.

Candyflower

WINDFLOWER
Anemone deltoidea
BUTTERCUP Family

Anemone probably comes from the Greek word *anemos,* meaning wind. The members of this genus supposedly open in response to spring-time breezes. A short-stemmed, white-flowered plant, windflower is common in shady, moist, sub-alpine woodlands and grows from 6 to 15 inches tall. It has two different types of leaves: a basal leaf that is deeply cleft into three parts and three simple, coarsely-toothed leaves on the stem. These are whorled, forming a triangle, as the species name deltoidea implies.

Anemone oregana is very similar and grows in the same type of area. However, the stem leaves are three-parted and the flowers range in color from pale blue to purple or lavender. It grows from 3 to 15 inches tall and is found in moist woods at moderate elevations. A more dainty anemone *(A. lyallii)* has flowers ranging in color from white to pink or blue. It is smaller (2 to 10 inches tall) with flowers only about ½ inch across. *Anemone oregana* is found in the Cascades of Washington and Oregon while *A. lyallii* may be found from British Columbia south into California.

Range: West of the Cascade crest in Washington (except on the Olympic Peninsula), Oregon, and northern California.

Oregon Anemone

Windflower

BANEBERRY
Actaea rubra
BUTTERCUP Family

Also called chinaberry. This perennial herb has an erect, branched stem, 1 to 3 feet tall, with 2 or 3 coarsely-toothed leaves that are divided several times. The tiny, white flowers, with numerous fine, thread-like stamens, are all borne in small round-topped clusters that open in June. However, it is when the fruits are ripe in July and August that baneberry is most noticeable. The bright red or pearly white berries resemble small china beads. They are mildly poisonous; however, many birds seem to be able to eat them without ill effects.

There are six species of *Actaea* in the northern temperate zone; however, this is the only one found in the Northwest.
Range: Widespread in North America.

Baneberry

Baneberry fruit

SHINING OREGON GRAPE
Berberis nervosa
BARBERRY Family

This plant also is called mountain Oregon grape, long-leafed Oregon grape, and holly grape. A showy plant up to two feet tall, this Oregon grape has yellow flowers that appear in May and June. It grows up to moderate elevations in the mountains, where it may be found along paths and trails winding through shady, subalpine forests. You can recognize it by its evergreen, leathery leaves, which consist of 11 to 21 spiny leaflets. *Berberis aquifolium,* the state flower of Oregon, is taller, growing 2 to 6 feet high, and is found at lower elevations. Its leaves consist of 5 to 9 leaflets.

The berries of both these species resemble grapes and make a fine jelly. Their juice may be sweetened with sugar. Both the juice and jelly taste very much like the products of the real wild grapes. The dried, yellow stems were used by the Indians as a dye, and the evergreen, holly-like leaves are often gathered and used for decoration.

Range: West of the Cascade crest from British Columbia south to central California.

Shining Oregon Grape

VANILLA-LEAF
Achlys triphylla
BARBERRY Family

Arising from a submerged rootstock, this plant may cover the ground for several square feet. The leaf is divided into three leaflets, the center one being triangular and the two lateral ones being somewhat fan-shaped. Lacking both petals and sepals, the flowers are composed only of white stamens and pistils. The leaves and flowering stem are 12 to 18 inches tall. Vanilla-leaf thrives in deep woodlands. The genus name comes from the Greek word meaning obscurity or night and perhaps refers to the dimly-lit areas where this plant grows.

The name vanilla-leaf refers to the odor of the leaves when they are being dried. The pleasant fragrance comes from a substance called coumarin. In fact, a vanilla substitute has been extracted from the leaves, but in such small amounts that it has no commercial value.

Range: British Columbia south through western Washington and Oregon to northwestern California.

Vanilla-leaf

COOLWORT
Tiarella unifoliata
SAXIFRAGE Family

This is a perennial herb, usually with only one simple, palmately-lobed leaf on each stem. Coolwort may grow singly or in clusters. The small, white flowers are borne on a slender stem about 18 inches tall. The stamens are longer than the sepals or thread-like petals, giving the flowers a dainty, lace-like appearance. Coolwort is found on the floor of moist woods and along streambanks at moderate elevations in the mountains. In some areas it is so plentiful that it nearly covers the ground, its white flowers looking like flecks of sunlight. The three-leafed coolwort *(T. trifoliata)* is similar, but its leaves are divided into three leaflets. Both bloom from June through September.

Range: Mountains from southern Alaska south to central California; also the northern Rocky Mountains.

Coolwort

MITREWORT
Mitella breweri
SAXIFRAGE Family

Also called bishop's cap. These tiny, pale-green flowers wave on a stalk less than one foot high in shaded areas of the montane forest. The flowers appear by June at moderate elevations in the Cascades, but may be found also near melting snowbanks under mountain hemlocks and subalpine firs at timberline in late August. All the leaves are basal, broad, and heart-shaped, with slightly wavy edges. The flower petals are so deeply cleft that they are thread-like. The fruit or capsule resembles a mitre (headband or cap worn by a bishop) and this gave rise to both the common and generic name.

Range: British Columbia south to the Olympic Mountains, through the Cascades to the central Sierra Nevada and east to the northern Rocky Mountains.

Mitrewort

SERVICEBERRY
Amelanchier alnifolia
ROSE Family

Also known as shadbush, shadblow, Juneberry, Saskatoon, and mountain pear. This serviceberry and its near relatives grow from the Atlantic to the Pacific. In the eastern states they bloom before the other woodland species have leaved out, providing a striking contrast to the otherwise bleak landscape.

In the Cascades it is a small tree, 15 to 20 feet tall; however, it may be more stunted at timberline. It may be recognized by its clusters of fragrant, white blossoms in early summer and the dark-colored fruit that follows. The leaves are rounded, and notched on the upper half. Although some find the berries a bit mealy, the sweet, deep blue fruit was a regular part of the Indians' diet. They dried them and pounded them into cakes for use in the winter, adding small bits to soups, stews, and vegetables. The Indians also made a concoction called pemmican by combining the berries with buffalo meat or venison. This was carried on long trips and was a favorite camp ration. The twigs and leaves are eaten by deer, elk, rabbits, and rodents. In some areas this small tree is extensively pruned from browsing by large mammals.

Range: Widespread in the mountains of the western states. Nearly a dozen species occur in North America.

Serviceberry

WILD ROSE
Rosa gymnocarpa
ROSE Family

A slender shrub 1 to 4 feet tall with sparse needle-like prickles, this dainty rose is one of the smallest in the Northwest and is fairly common in moist forests throughout the Cascades. It has five-petaled pink flowers, about one inch in diameter, and leaves with 5 to 9 roundish leaflets. The fruit is bright red, barely a half-inch in diameter.

Rose fruits, called hips, have been called one of the finest sources of vitamin C available in the world. During World War II authorities in both England and the Scandinavian countries used the fruits extensively when citrus was nearly impossible to get. It was substituted for oranges in the diet. Rose hips make excellent jams and jellies, although one should wait until after the first frost before picking them.

The Indians used the wild rose for a variety of purposes. They made a hot beverage for colds from the tender roots; they used the leaves and hips to make a drink to cure colics, and a mixture from the cooked seeds to alleviate muscular pains. They also used straight stems for arrow shafts. Wild rose hips are eaten regularly by grouse, quail, bear, and other forms of wildlife. Since the fruit remains on the bush throughout the winter, it is a good emergency food supply for wild animals.

Range: Widespread throughout the Northwest, east to the Continental Divide.

Wild Rose

DWARF BRAMBLE
Rubus lasiococcus
ROSE Family

The dwarf bramble spreads by runners as well as seeds. Roots develop along the creeping stems, and a new plant arises. Sometimes the creamy-white petals of the raspberry-like flowers are hidden under the club-shaped leaves as the plant trails across abandoned roads, over wooded clearings, and along trails in mountain woodlands.

Trailing raspberry, *Rubus pedatus,* is similar to the dwarf bramble and has white flowers. However, its leaves are divided into 3 to 5 leaflets while those of the dwarf bramble are merely lobed.

Both these plants are found from the lowlands to the higher elevations. *Rubus,* meaning red, denotes the color of the fruit in all the *Rubus* discussed here. These fruits, similar to those of a red raspberry, are edible. (Also see pages 66, 67.)

Range: Cascades from northern California to British Columbia; also the Olympic Mountains.

WOOD SORREL
Oxalis oregana
OXALIS Family

Wood sorrel, which completely covers parts of the forest floor in the lower mountain valleys, is recognized easily by its clover-shaped leaves, which fold at night and droop in strong sunlight. The leaves are very palatable, eaten eagerly by youngsters who maintain that they taste somewhat like strawberries. In addition, the leaves make excellent salad greens. As their name implies, they contain oxalic acid.

A very similar species, *O. trilliifolia,* often grows amidst the wood sorrel. You can distinguish it because more than one flower may be found on each stem. *Oxalis oregana* has only one white (or, sometimes, pink) flower per stem and grows about 4 to 6 inches tall; *O. trilliifolia* is a little taller, growing up to 10 inches tall and has white or cream-colored flowers.

Range: From Washington south to central California, from the coast east through the Cascades.

WOOD VIOLET
Viola glabella
VIOLET Family

Also called johnny jump-up. This is probably the most common of the yellow violets found from the lowland valleys up into the higher elevations, where it appears as the snowbanks melt. It is also one of the largest of the Northwestern violets, growing nearly a foot tall. It has heart-shaped leaves and is common in moist woodland areas.

Many other violets are also found in the Cascades. Another yellow violet with circular instead of heart-shaped leaves, is the round-leaved violet, *V. orbiculata.* It occurs in the Olympic and Cascade Mountains as well as the mountains of Idaho and Montana. It is found mainly above 4,000 feet elevation. A blue violet that occurs throughout most of western North America, is the western long-spurred violet, *V. adunca.* The lower petal of all violets develops backward, forming a small sac or spur. In the western long-spurred violet, this sac is half as long as the flower itself. A very tiny white violet found in high elevation bogs and wet meadows throughout the Cascades and other mountain ranges in the western states is Macloskey's violet, *V. macloskeyi.* Its stems are barely 3 or 4 inches tall.

In violets, the first flowers to bloom are sometimes sterile and do not produce seeds. These are the showy blossoms commonly observed. After they fall, small green flowers are produced next to the ground. These often develop more seeds than the earlier, showy flowers.

Range: Mountains of the Pacific states, east to the northern Rockies. Also found in northeast Asia.

41

Wood Violet

BUNCHBERRY
Cornus canadensis
DOGWOOD Family

Also called dwarf cornel or dwarf dogwood. The easily recognized bunchberry often covers the forest floor at moderate elevations in the Cascades where it is associated with the hemlocks, Douglas fir, and western white pine. The 4 to 8 inch stem appears to be topped by a single white flower. Actually, the "petals" are bracts and the true flowers are small yellow structures in the center of the petal-like bracts. The flowers bloom in June and, in some areas, may still be found in August. The flowers are followed by a clump of bright red berries referred to by the common name. These berries are edible and were used to some extent by various Indian tribes in North America.

Range: Widespread in the western mountains and across northern North America; also Asia.

Bunchberry

PACIFIC DOGWOOD
Cornus nuttallii
DOGWOOD Family

The dogwood is one of our most attractive flowering trees, being found at moderate elevations in the Cascades. It grows in the shade of Douglas firs and western hemlocks, or on the edge of a stream or the forest, where its clean white bracts are even more conspicuous. This small tree flowers in April and May, although the bracts may hang on well into June at higher elevations. It is also colorful in the fall when bright red berries replace the flowers, and the foliage turns an attractive red. These characteristics make this a desirable garden species.

The Pacific dogwood was first recognized as a new species by the botanist Thomas Nuttall. When he first observed the tree, he thought it was a western magnolia. Previous observers had assumed it to be the same species as the eastern dogwood. Nuttall was in the company of Dr. John Townsend, an ornithologist and physician at Ft. Vancouver in 1835. At that time two children of the nearby Cowlitz Indian tribe were sick with a fever. Dr. Townsend recognized the malaria and treated it with an extract from the dogwood bark. The eastern dogwood had long been used as a quinine substitute. *Range:* British Columbia south on the western side of the Cascades to California; also in the northern mountains of Idaho.

PRINCE'S PINE
Chimaphila umbellata
HEATH Family

Also called pipsissewa and wintergreen. Found on the floor of conifer forests, this plant has loosely whorled, leathery, toothed leaves and grows from 5 to 10 inches tall. It has waxy-petaled flowers, ranging in color from pink to white, clustered at the top of the stem and appearing in May, June, or July, depending on elevation. *Chimaphila* means winter-loving in Greek, and refers to its evergreen leaves, which retain their color throughout the winter. The name may also allude to the cool forests where this genus is usually found.

One other member of this genus is found in the Northwest: *Chimaphila menziesii*. It is smaller, growing from 3 to 6 inches tall, and has fewer flowers and leaves. The leaves are oval, while those of *Chimaphila umbellata* are lance-shaped.

Range: Widespread in northern and western North America; also Eurasia.

44

PINEDROPS
Pterospora andromedea
HEATH Family

This is the tallest of the saprophytes (plants that derive their nourishment from decaying plant material) growing in the Northwest and is usually found in association with the ponderosa pines on the eastern side of the Cascades. The plant grows from 1 to 3 feet tall and consists of one or more stems with bell-shaped flowers hanging from the upper portion. There are no green leaves on the plant, these having been reduced to brownish scales along the stem, which is red or brown.

The stalks are sometimes gathered in late summer and used in floral decorations, since the dried plant holds well throughout the winter. They are conspicuous plants growing among the dried pine needles covering the forest floor.

The roots of this plant, like those of the pinesap and Indian pipe (page 46), are closely associated with the fungi that decay fallen organic material. The fungi reduces the decaying material and then the roots of the pinedrops absorb the decayed matter. Pinedrops' association with fungi has allowed it to utilize a mode of nutrition not used by green plants.

Range: Widespread in the western states, east across North America to Labrador and Pennsylvania.

Pinedrops

PINESAP
Hypopitys monotropa
HEATH Family

Arising from a dense mass of fleshy roots, these succulent plants are saprophytes. The whole plant is reddish or yellow, with leaves represented by small, flattened scales along the stem. The flowers are borne in a one-sided cluster at the tip of each stem. When the stem emerges from the forest duff, the pendant flowers are crowded at the tip of the stem. The flowers become erect as the plant matures. Growing up to a foot tall, pinesap occurs mainly on the floor of damp conifer woods, commonly growing from decaying stumps and logs.

Indian pipe *(Monotropa uniflora)* is closely related and has a single flower at the tip of each stem, resembling a white wax pipe planted in the ground. Growing 4 to 10 inches tall, it is also found in damp, conifer forests. When the plant is fresh, it is a ghostly-white color. However, it turns black upon wilting or drying. Other names, including ghost pipe, corpse plant, and ghost flower, denote the color and texture of the stems.

Both of these scientific names tell us a bit about the plants. The name *Hypopitys* comes from the Greek *hypo* (beneath) and *pitys* (pine tree), referring to the evergreen forests where these plants are found. The Greek words *monos* (one) and *tropos* (direction) allude to the drooping flowers, turned to one side, typical of both plants. The word uniflora, however, tells us that only one flower is found on each Indian pipe stem.

Range: British Columbia south through California and east across northern North America to the Atlantic.

Pinesap

PACIFIC RHODODENDRON
Rhododendron macrophyllum
HEATH Family

The state flower of Washington, this spectacular shrub blooms from May to July, depending on elevation. Many towns along the Pacific coast and in the Cascade foothills are so blessed with these plants that they hold festivals during the peak of their blooming period. The blossoms may form clumps 6 inches or more across, providing a display of color unequaled by any other native shrub. The genus name is derived from the Greek for rose tree, thus describing the beautiful red and pink blossoms of this member of the genus. It has been widely cultivated and bred for particular color and flower size. The native plant grows from 5 to 10 feet tall, although it is often a low, sprawling shrub, and bears pale pink or deep rose-colored flowers. Its leaves are leathery and oblong, with edges that are rolled slightly under.

Early settlers to the Northwest called this shrub a laurel, confusing it with closely-related eastern shrubs. They did not generally appreciate its beauty. The members of the Barlow party, the first to cross the southern flanks of Mt. Hood, named a steep slope after it—Laurel Hill. To them the shrubs represented dense thickets and the tangled branches hindered travel.

Range: British Columbia through western Washington and Oregon, south along the coast to central California.

Pacific Rhododendron

FOOL'S HUCKLEBERRY
Menziesia ferruginea
HEATH Family

Also called rusty huckleberry (because its flowers are rust-colored) and false azalea. This common shrub, about 3 to 6 feet tall, is found at moderate altitudes throughout the Cascades. The plant somewhat resembles the huckleberry bush, to which it is related. However, the dry, woody fruits are not edible and account for the common name fool's huckleberry. Its leaves are covered with fine hairs on both the upper and lower surfaces. Young twigs are a rusty color, as are the bell-shaped flowers that hang on a long stem and are often hidden among the leaves. Fool's huckleberry occurs as the understory of open conifer woods, usually associated with elderberry, Douglas fir, Pacific rhododendron, and the true huckleberries. The plant was named for Archibald Menzies, a surgeon and naturalist with Vancouver's Pacific Coast expedition from 1790 to 1795. He was one of the first botanists to study the plants of the Pacific Northwest.

Range: Along the coast and in the Cascades, from southern Alaska to central California, east to the mountains of Montana.

ONE-SIDED PYROLA
Pyrola secunda
HEATH Family

Also called shinleaf, side-bells. There are several species of pyrola in the Cascades. They range from a few inches to over a foot in height. The pale green, cream, or pink-colored flowers are arranged along the stem and droop downward, hanging like bells. The basal leaves are evergreen in most cases and slightly leathery-textured.

One-sided pyrola can be recognized because all the flowers are borne on one side of the stem. Growing about 6 or 8 inches tall, it is one of the most common pyrolas found in our area, although it may be overlooked because its flowers are a drab green or white. It grows on the damp forest floor of conifer forests at moderate elevations in the mountains.

Another easily recognized pyrola is the white-veined pyrola, *P. picta.* It is found in drier situations and prominent, white veins mark its leathery leaves. Growing 6 to 12 inches tall, its flowers are pale pink or white. A pyrola with pinkish or dull red flowers, leathery shinleaf *(P. bracteata)* grows about 8 to 15 inches tall and may be found in open, dry conifer woods, often growing on shaded rocky outcrops. This is the largest and most robust of our pyrolas. The leaves are round or ovate, forming a rosette at the base of the plant.

Once included in this genus but now thought to be in a genus by itself, *Moneses uniflora,* commonly called single beauty, closely resembles the prince's pine (see page 44). Its leaves are similar to those of pyrolas. However, it has only one cream-colored saucer-shaped flower atop its short (2 to 6 inch) stem, while pyrolas and prince's pine have more than one.

Range: Widespread in North America and Eurasia.

White-veined Pyrola

One-sided Pyrola

SALAL
Gaultheria shallon
HEATH Family

A common shrub with shining, oval leaves and white, bell-shaped flowers, salal may grow 1 to 7 feet tall. The evergreen leaves are from 2 to 4 inches long. The flowers bloom from mid-May through mid-July, depending on elevation and are followed by dark blue berries, highly prized by the Indians. These utilitarian fruits were gathered and made into syrup or dried and ground into flour and stored as flat cakes. The fresh berries were later used by the settlers for pies and jams; they are greatly relished by birds, small mammals, and bears. The Scottish botanist David Douglas considered this to be one of his favorite plants. He hoped to cultivate the plant for its fruit. While this has not been done, salal has been widely planted in England as an ornamental.

Gaultheria ovatifolia is a creeping ground plant with oval, evergreen leaves that are such a deep green they almost look black. The tiny white, bell-shaped flowers are hidden in the axils of the leathery leaves, which are themselves only about an inch long. Both these *Gaultheria* grow up to middle elevations in the mountains.

Range: Southern Alaska south through California on the western side of the Cascades.

Salal

BLACK HUCKLEBERRY
Vaccinium membranaceum
HEATH Family

Also called whortleberry. The Indians waited eagerly for the ripening of this close relative of the cultivated blueberry. Growing on a low shrub, 2 to 5 feet tall, the inconspicuous, green flower is bell-shaped, like so many other members of the heath family. The flower is rarely seen. However, the blue-black berry is well-known. It ripens in August or September, depending on altitude. Growing at lower elevations in the mountains, *V. ovalifolium* also produces excellent fruit. This shrub grows 6 feet or more, and the berry has a whitish bloom (waxy coating).

Whole tribes of Indians once migrated to the high meadows to gather huckleberries. The Still Creek area on Mt. Hood was a favored camping spot, and still hums with activity in August when the fruit in the nearby Sherar Burn area is ripe. The Klamath Indians regularly trekked to a spot called Huckleberry Mountain in the southern Oregon Cascades to harvest the fruit. Migrations still occur as thousands of "flat-landers" swarm to the Cascades to pick the tasty berries.

The black huckleberry is often found in open, burned over areas, popular spots for berry-pickers. Before fire, however, this huckleberry is normally found growing beneath stately trees in the conifer forests covering the Cascades. Large acreages of forest have been burned over during the past years. The fire-resistant huckleberry remains after the burn and thus may be the dominant plant over acres of open space. Eventually, the larger trees re-seed and grow up through the huckleberry; the forest is re-established.

Range: High mountains from British Columbia to northern California, east to the northern Rocky Mountains.

Black Huckleberry

STARFLOWER
Trientalis latifolia
PRIMROSE Family

One look at the white, pointed petals making up this symmetrical little flower tells the origin of the name. The entire plant is barely 4 to 8 inches high and has 3 to 6 ovate stem leaves occurring in a whorl below the white flowers. Look for it along shaded roadsides and meadow borders or beneath dense stands of Douglas fir or hemlock.

Another species of starflower in the Northwest is *Trientalis arctica*. It is much smaller, being just a few inches tall. Its white flowers are about one-half inch across and its leaves scattered along the entire length of the stem. It grows in bogs and wet areas such as Kinzel Lake in the Mt. Hood National Forest.

Range: British Columbia south along the coast and western Cascades and Sierra Nevada to central California.

Starflower

PARROTBEAK
Pedicularis racemosa
FIGWORT Family

Also called sickletop louse-wort. Like its close relative, elephant head (see page 115), the shape of the flowers on this plant has resulted in a descriptive name. The pale pink or white flowers have two lips, the upper one is extended and curves down to the lower one, looking like a distinct beak. The linear leaves are purple tinged and have doubly toothed edges. Parrotbeak grows from 6 to 18 inches tall and is very common in the ponderosa pine forests of the eastern Cascades and in the moist woodlands and openings of moderate elevations in the western Cascades.

Range: Widespread in the mountains of western North America.

Parrotbeak

TWINFLOWER
Linnaea borealis
HONEYSUCKLE Family

A low-growing plant with small evergreen leaves, twinflower's pink, bell-shaped flowers hang from short stalks. In June and July slender stems shoot 2 to 4 inches above the woody vines and are soon adorned with pairs of fragrant blossoms. Twinflower's thin, spreading vines creep over the ground at moderate elevations in the Cascade Mountains and may carpet large areas of the forest floor with shiny, leathery leaves. One usually does not have to walk far in the woods before coming across this plant growing in the cool shade beneath Douglas fir and stately hemlocks.

Twinflower was named for the Swedish scientist Carolus Linnaeus (1707-1778), who was largely responsible for the development of the binomial system of naming plants and animals. Each individual has a generic and specific name, and these two Latin words become the scientific name.

Range: Circumpolar, widespread across the northern areas of North America and in the mountains of the western United States.

Twinflower

DRY OPENINGS IN CONIFEROUS FORESTS

BEARGRASS
Xerophyllum tenax
LILY Family

Also called squawgrass, elkgrass. One of the most conspicuous of the mountain wildflowers, beargrass lines the road to Timberline Lodge on Mt. Hood during June and covers meadows along the Pacific Crest Trail. It has a dense clump of grass-like leaves at its base and a plume of white flowers atop a 2 to 5 foot tall stalk. Since individual plants may not bloom every year, the flowers may be very abundant one year, almost absent the next.

The name squawgrass results from the Indians' use of the grass-like leaves for weaving baskets and clothing, the work of the squaws in the tribe. Squawgrass was so important that it was even used as an article of trade by the Indians, who constructed baskets, hats, pouches, and even water-tight cooking pots from the coarse leaves. The Indians often colored some of the bear-grass with various plant dyes, weaving it into basket designs. The names elkgrass and bear-grass come from the fact that these animals sometimes eat a great deal of this plant. Bears particularly like the succulent base of the plant, which is very tender in the spring. Small rodents are also known to chew on the plant.

Range: In the high mountains from the northern Rocky Mountains west to the Pacific states. In Oregon it is absent in the southern Cascades around Crater Lake, but is found in isolated areas of the coast mountains. Beargrass also occurs in the Sierra Nevada of California.

Beargrass

WASHINGTON LILY
Lilium washingtonianum
LILY Family

An upright plant 3 to 6 feet tall, the Washington lily, strangely enough, is not found north of the Columbia River, but grows at moderate elevations in the Oregon and California Cascades and northern Sierra Nevada, where it is known by local names such as Mt. Hood lily, Shasta lily, and Santiam lily. Over much of its range it has been picked so indiscriminately that it is now difficult to find. However, where it occurs it is easy to recognize because it resembles an Easter lily. The white blossoms turn pink with age and are extremely fragrant.

Range: Columbia River south through the Cascades to the northern Sierra Nevada.

Washington Lily

LARKSPUR
Delphinium glareosum
BUTTERCUP Family

The deep blue flowers of the larkspur are easy to recognize, and some species of *Delphinium* are cultivated in gardens. The flower has always been the subject of ill will with the rancher, however, because it is poisonous to cattle. The young shoots in the spring are considered to be especially toxic. Domestic sheep do not seem to be affected by the larkspur, and so are sometimes grazed in cattle range simply to rid the area of this plant. The main poison is an alkaloid, which has doubled as a remedy for various ailments and has been used externally to kill parasites.

The larkspur's beauty cannot be disputed and a hillside covered with these flowers is a sight to remember. There are about 200 species of larkspur in North America; more than 20 in the Northwest. You can recognize a larkspur plant by the irregularly lobed or divided leaves and odd-shaped flowers, which have 5 blue or purple petal-like sepals, the upper one spurred backward. Occasionally pink or white flowers are found. Often different species are difficult to tell apart. This species stands about one foot tall and thrives on partially shaded alpine and sub-alpine talus slopes and meadows. Its lower petals are deeply notched.

Range: Cascades from central Washington to central Oregon; also the Olympic Mountains.

Larkspur

WILD BLEEDING HEART
Dicentra formosa
BLEEDING HEART Family

Wild bleeding heart, which resembles its cultivated city cousin, blooms in cool, sheltered places as soon as the snow melts. The flowers have four, rose-colored petals forming a heart-shaped sack with two spurs at the base. The flowering stalk is from 10 to 20 inches tall, standing slightly above the leaves, which are cut into many narrow segments resembling lace-work. This genus contains alkaloids that are poisonous to many animals. However, since the leaves are not very palatable, very few animals eat them.

Range: Coast to mid-elevations of the Cascades, from western British Columbia to central California.

CREAMY STONECROP
Sedum oregonense
STONECROP Family

Blooming in open rocky areas, stonecrops are recognized by their star-shaped flowers and thickened leaves. The leaves are fleshy and seem to cling to the rocks on which they are found. Acting like the succulent tissue of a cactus, the leaves store water to be used during dry periods. In this species, a tuft of creamy flowers adorns the 3 to 8 inch stems. Most of the leaves are borne in a rosette at the base of the stems and, nearly an inch long, are roughly oblong or spatulate. A few smaller leaves are found alternately on the stem. (See page 134 for a description of another stonecrop.)

There are nearly 400 species of stonecrop in the world; most of them occur in northern areas, but a few are found south of the equator in mountainous regions. About a dozen occur in the Pacific Northwest.

Range: Cascades of Oregon, Washington, and northern California.

Creamy Stonecrop

STICKY CURRANT
Ribes viscosissimum
SAXIFRAGE Family

Small shrubs (1 to 3 feet tall) with glandular, sticky leaves, this *Ribes* is common in both the Cascades and the Rocky Mountains. It is found from moderate elevations to timberline areas. The whitish, bell-shaped flowers are followed by black fruits. This genus includes all the wild and domestic currants and gooseberries, which are excellent eating, either fresh or cooked into pies and jellies. The currants may be distinguished from the gooseberries because they lack spines while gooseberry stems are usually covered with them.

Another *Ribes* common in the Cascades is *Ribes howellii,* which has saucer-shaped flowers. It forms dense thickets below and up to timberline. The small flowers are a pale purple color. The brilliant red-flowering currant *(R. sanguineum)* is very conspicuous in lowland areas in the spring. It occurs along the coast and in wooded valleys throughout the Cascades.

Range: Widespread in the mountains of the western states.

Sticky Currant

MOUNTAIN ASH
Sorbus sitchensis
ROSE Family

The mountain ash, with its almost flat-topped cluster of white flowers, sprinkles the subalpine forest with its beauty in early spring. Look for it along roadsides and meadow openings. It is not a large tree and rarely reaches 20 feet; at timberline it may not grow above 2 or 3 feet tall. Its leaves consist of 7 to 11 leaflets, toothed only on the terminal half. During the later part of the summer this tree is covered by clusters of brightly-colored berries. These fruits are eaten by many birds, especially by the varied thrush that is so common in the Cascades. They were also gathered by the early settlers when other food was not available and were ground into a meal or made into jams and jellies. The showy white flowers and orange-red berries make the mountain ash popular as an ornamental, and it can be found in many lowland yards and gardens.

Range: Mountains of Alaska through Oregon, northern California, and Montana.

Mountain Ash

Mountain Ash fruit

64

FIELD STRAWBERRY
Fragaria vesca
ROSE Family

The wild strawberry is renowned for its tasty, if dainty, goodness. Although many blossoms may cover the ground, sometimes berries are hard to find. Grouse, rabbits, robins, small rodents, and bears all consume them eagerly. The fruit was cherished by the Indians, who gathered the sweet-tasting berries. They also utilized the leaves for making a hot beverage.

There are several species of wild strawberry in the Northwest. Like the others, this species has a three-parted leaf. These leaves are not leathery, however, like those of the coastal strawberry, but thin and smooth, bright green above and pale beneath. Each plant sends out numerous stolons—"runners" that lie across the ground and root, producing new plants.

Range: Widespread in Europe and North America.

Field Strawberry

THIMBLEBERRY
Rubus parviflorus
ROSE Family

Lining roadsides and openings up to moderate elevations in the mountains and along the coast, thimbleberry owes its name to the shape of its berries, which resemble pale raspberries and are thimble-shaped. Generally their flavor is rather bland, but the Indians ate them readily. A low shrub, thimbleberry grows 3 to 6 feet high. The five white floral petals have the texture of thin, crinkled paper, while the broadly-lobed maple-like leaves feel more like rough velvet. The tender young shoots were eaten by the Indians, while the leaves and stems are sometimes eaten by both the black-tailed and mule deer. (Also see pages 39, 67.)
Range: Alaska east to Ontario and the Great Lakes, south to California and New Mexico.

Thimbleberry

SALMONBERRY
Rubus spectabilis
ROSE Family

In contrast to *Rubus parvi-florus,* this shrub has reddish flowers and instead of a broad, entire leaf, has leaves divided into three coarsely-toothed leaflets. It is a very common shrub along woodland openings and roadsides at moderate elevations and grows from 3 to 12 feet tall, depending on soil conditions and elevations. Salmonberry has small thorns on its stems, and where it has favorable growing conditions, can produce an impenetrable thicket. The tangled bushes therefore provide excellent protection for nesting birds and shelter for small rodents.

Depending on elevation, the nearly 1 inch wide flowers appear from April to June. Often, a shrub will produce new buds while flowering so it is possible to have some fruit on the plant while new flowers are opening. Sometimes the ground beneath will be covered with the rose-red flower petals because they often fall with the slightest touch or breeze. The berries come in two colors: a clear orange, and a deeper red. While the deep red berry may be prettier to look at, many hikers think the orange one has more taste to it.

Some sources say the plant gets its name because the lighter colored berries resemble a cluster of salmon eggs. There are other stories for the origin of the name. One concerns a remedy made from its bark that early settlers and the Indians used to cure a disorder caused by eating too many salmon.

Range: Throughout the Pacific Northwest, west of the Cascade crest.

DRUMMOND'S CINQUEFOIL
Potentilla drummondii
ROSE Family

The cinquefoils resemble buttercups, having 5 yellow petals surrounding a dark center. (See page 136 for the differences between buttercups and cinquefoils.)

Commonly found in subalpine meadows and forest openings, this cinquefoil grows from 8 to 16 inches tall. Its stems grow in small clumps and bear long-petioled basal leaves with from 5 to 9 deeply-toothed leaflets. The leaves are pinnately compound (the leaflets arranged along the sides of the leaf petiole, like the parts of a feather). The slender cinquefoil *(P. gracilis)* grows from 1 to 2 feet tall and has from 5 to 7 leaflets arranged palmately (all the leaflets arise from a common point, spreading like the fingers of a hand). The lower surface of the leaflets are covered with thin white hairs.

Range: Cascade Mountains from British Columbia through the Sierra Nevada of California; also the Rocky Mountains and the Olympic Mountains.

Drummond's Cinquefoil

SUBALPINE SPIREA
Spiraea betulifolia
ROSE Family

Also called birch-leafed spirea. This woody shrub, which is usually prostrate, sending up erect, leafy stems 1 or 2 feet tall, is identified by a white, flat-topped crown of flowers that may be 4 inches across. Because each flower has numerous stamens extending beyond the other floral parts, the flower cluster has a soft, fuzzy appearance. The stems are reddish in color and somewhat brittle. This spirea is often seen along roadsides, on rocky bluffs, and in dry, open forests at moderate elevations in the Cascades. There it is commonly associated with Douglas fir and lodgepole pine forests.

Range: British Columbia south through the Cascades to central Oregon, east to Wyoming and North Dakota. Also found in Asia.

Subalpine Spirea

OCEAN SPRAY
Holodiscus discolor
ROSE Family

Also called arrow-wood, creambush, mountain spray. A shrub 3 to 20 feet high with wedge-shaped, toothed or lobed leaves, ocean spray is covered by drooping tassels of tightly-clustered white flowers. They generally bloom in June and July, depending on elevation, and abound along roads, streambanks, canyons, and woodland openings. Ocean spray is found along the coast as well as at moderate elevations in the mountains. This plant derives its name from the beautiful plume of white flowers that may remind one of the foamy spray of the ocean surf. Its beauty has earned it a place in many Northwestern gardens. It was also a valuable plant for the Indians—they made arrow shafts from the straight young shoots.

Range: British Columbia south through central California, east in the mountains to western Montana.

Ocean Spray

GOAT'S BEARD
Aruncus sylvester
ROSE Family

This showy, cosmopolitan plant is found only at the lower elevations and could be confused with ocean spray, since it also has plumes of white flowers. However, its leaves are divided two or three times, while those of ocean spray are simple. The flowers turn a dull yellow or brown as they wither. Although 3 to 7 feet tall and usually thought of as a shrub, goat's beard dies back each year, sending out new, fast-growing shoots in the spring. It is not a shrub because it lacks definite woody tissue above the ground. The name goat's beard describes the hanging white flowers, which resemble a white beard. Look for it as you drive through the cool forests along the Santiam Highway of Oregon, or the Mather Memorial Parkway leading into Mt. Rainier National Park.

Range: Moist woods throughout Europe, Asia, Japan, and across the northern portion o' North America.

Goat's Beard

SUBALPINE LUPINE
Lupinus latifolius
PEA Family

Lupines as a group are a well-known and showy segment of the alpine flora. They often carpet whole slopes with blue to purple color; they are common beneath dense stands of lodgepole pine, where few other flowers grow; they often line roadsides and trails in the high country. *Lupinus latifolius* is especially abundant around Mt. Hood, Mt. Adams and the Three Sisters. It is a bushy plant, 1 to 2 feet tall, abounding in both open areas and partial shade. At lower elevations it may grow taller. The flowers are about a half inch long and are deep purple with a white center area. Farther south it is largely replaced by Anderson's Lupine, *Lupinus andersonii,* which lines the roads in Crater Lake National Park and is also common at Lassen Volcanic National Park.

It was once thought that the lupine robbed the soil of nutrients because it grew in dry, rocky, barren areas where other plants could not survive. So the country folk supposed it to be like the wolf, which they felt robbed their chicken yards. This may be how the genus name originated— *Lupinus* is derived from the word *lupus,* meaning wolf. In actuality, lupines grow in such areas because they fertilize the soil where they take root and are not dependent on fertile soil to survive. Like other members of the pea family, the lupines have small nodules on their roots. These contain bacteria that take free nitrogen from the air, converting it to soil nitrogen. Since *Lupinus* fertilizes the soil in which it grows, it can grow where other plants cannot.

Range: Alaska south in the mountains through British Columbia to the Cascades of Oregon and northern California.

SNOWBUSH
Ceanothus velutinus
BUCKTHORN Family

Also called sticky laurel and white lilac. This evergreen, 2 to 5 foot tall shrub covers clear-cuts and roadways at middle altitudes in the Cascades. *Ceanothus* blooming on a hillside looks like fresh snow. The leaves are very glossy above, slightly hairy below—the species name means velvety. The entire plant has a pleasant, aromatic odor, especially after a rain. Dense growths of snowbush may carpet a hillside, the branches forming an impenetrable tangle. A hiker can slide down the slope, over the branches, but it is extremely difficult to try to climb uphill over them.

Many species of *Ceanothus* contain saponin, which gives the flowers and fruits soap-like qualities. Both the Indians and pioneers used the flowers as a soap substitute.

Range: British Columbia south along the coast and in the Cascades to California, east to the northern Rocky Mountains.

Snowbush

FIREWEED
Epilobium angustifolium
EVENING PRIMROSE Family

Fireweed is easily recognized —tall plumes of pink, four-petaled flowers on stems up to 7 feet tall. The stems are covered with spear-shaped leaves, a trait referred to by the species name. The flowers bloom from the bottom of the stalk upward, a trait characteristic of plants with flowers growing in racemes (flower clusters with the flowers arranged linearly along a stem, each individual flower on its own tiny stalk). Perhaps this method of flowering is to insure that an opening bud will not be shaded by a flower above it. Usually you can see the pod-like fruits, flowers, and unopened buds all on the same plant. The long, tubular seed-pods split into ribbon-like sections, releasing tiny seeds. These are carried to new areas by tufts of silky hairs that act like a parachute. A light breeze is enough to carry the seeds to recently disturbed areas such as road-cuts, clear-cuts, abandoned fields, and burned-over wood-lands. The name fireweed comes from the fact that this plant is so prominent in recently burned areas. They may cover entire fields and hillsides with red color, another good reason to call the plant fireweed.

This plant is a valuable range plant, being eaten by both deer and elk as well as live-stock. In Europe and Asia tender young shoots are prepared and eaten like asparagus. The Canadians also utilize it like a vegetable. To those who keep bees it is very desirable because it makes excellent honey.

Range: Low valleys to timber-line in western and northern North America, Europe, and Asia.

Fireweed

WHITE RHODODENDRON
Rhododendron albiflorum
HEATH Family

Also called Cascades azalea and mountain misery—this last name coming from its tangle of branches, hindering the progress of hikers near timberline. A thin-leaved shrub about 6 feet tall, this bush grows to timberline, but is also common in the moderate elevation forest borders. The creamy-white flowers, about an inch across, grow in small, compact clusters among the leaves at the end of each branch. The flowers later dry and their brownish remains may hang on the branch until the following spring.

Range: Mountains of British Columbia, Washington and Oregon, east to the northern Rockies.

75

PINEMAT MANZANITA
Arcotaphylos nevadensis
HEATH Family

A low, sprawling red-barked shrub seldom over a foot high, this manzanita is common from moderate altitudes to near timberline in the Cascades. It has white, urn-shaped flowers and round, red berries. Several other manzanitas also occur in the Oregon Cascades. Another low, mat-forming species is the bearberry *(A. uva-ursi),* also called kinnikinnick, which has pinkish flowers and is widespread in western and northern North America. Found at lower elevations, the hairy manzanita *(A. columbiana)* is a shrub growing between 2 and 9 feet tall, being especially abundant in the southern Cascades. Its stem and leaves are covered with stiff, bristle-like hairs. It grows along the coast and in the lower Cascades from British Columbia to central California. Greenleaf manzanita *(A. patula)* is a 3 to 8 foot tall shrub and lacks the stiff hairs of *A. columbiana.* It is very common in the southern Cascades, where it may form dense thickets under ponderosa pine forests. It lines the Cleetwood Cove Trail at Crater Lake National Park and is common in the lower areas of the Deschutes National Forest.

There are over 45 species of manzanita and most of them occur in the Pacific coastal states, especially California. All have glossy, evergreen leaves and hanging, urn-shaped flowers. The older and taller shrubs have peeling red bark and extremely crooked branches. For this reason they have been collected for decorative lamp stands and other artistic endeavors. The Indians' use of this group of plants was more utilitarian.

They had many uses for the small fruits, red berries. (The name manzanita is Spanish for little apple.) The Indians ate the berries raw, stewed, boiled, or ground into a powder. They also made a cider from them, first crushing them and adding hot water. The brew was cooled and drunk. The California Indians ranked the berries with acorns and pinyon nuts as valuable food items. There were still other uses for the manzanita. A solution made from the berries was used for curing poison oak, and the crushed leaves were dried and mixed with tobacco for smoking. The hard wood was used by the early California settlers as pegs in place of iron nails.

Range: Mountains of B.C. south to northern California.

Pinemat Manzanita

SPREADING DOGBANE
Apocynum androsaemifolium
DOGBANE Family

Generally found on dry hill-sides and along roads, this plant is usually less than 1 or 2 feet tall, with pinkish-white flowers. The drab, open areas it inhabits make dogbane conspicuous. The egg-shaped leaves are rather thick to the touch and arranged opposite each other on the stem. Since the individual flowers bloom at different times, a single plant may bloom from May through July. A very good grade of honey can be derived from the fragrant flowers. A milky juice exudes when the smooth, red stem is broken. After the juice hardens, it has properties similar to rubber. This plant is closely related to the Indian hemp used by various Indians in making nets and ropes.
Range: Most of North America, except the southeastern United States.

Spreading Dogbane

JACOB'S LADDER
Polemonium californicum
PHLOX Family

Named because the arrangement of the leaflets resembles a ladder, Jacob's ladder grows 6 to 10 inches tall. It may be found under the partial shade of mountain hemlocks, sometimes even venturing onto the open grassy slopes above timberline. The funnel-shaped flowers impart a light blue color to the landscape. Another species, *P. pulcherrimum,* may also be found. It is smaller, about 4 or 6 inches tall, and its terminal leaflets are completely separate, while those of *P. californicum* are fused. However, some authorities believe this and other differences in size and flower structure are simply variations of the same species.

Range: Olympic, Cascade, and Siskiyou Mountains. Also extends south to central Sierra Nevada.

78

SKYROCKET GILIA
Gilia aggregata
PHLOX Family

Also called scarlet gilia, foxfire. Even though alpine areas are known for their vivid, bright-colored flowers, nothing else in the Cascades can match the brilliant scarlet of this gilia. Thin, tubular flowers nearly an inch long flare out with five scarlet petals. Where whole alpine meadows are aglow with these blossoms, every other type of flower seems pale. The whole plant consists of a 1 to 3 foot tall stem with much-divided leaves. It is found from low to high elevations in forest openings and meadows in the mountains. Look for skyrocket gilia around Booth Lake near Three-fingered Jack, in Castle Crest Wildflower Garden in Crater Lake National Park, and in the Grassy Swale area at Lassen Volcanic National Park in June and July.

Range: Widespread in the mountains of western North America; in the Pacific Northwest, mainly east of the Cascade crest.

Skyrocket Gilia

HEDGENETTLE
Stachys cooleyae
MINT Family

A common member of the mint family, hedgenettle frequents open areas and roadsides at lower elevations where it may cover large areas. It is a coarse plant, growing 2 to 6 feet high, and has opposite leaves. These leaves are covered with fine hairs, and, although resembling the leaves of the fragrant garden mints, have a strong, rank odor, especially when crushed. The tubular, bright red flowers are two-lipped, and the lower lip is spotted with white flecks. These showy flowers, often more than an inch long, are clustered in a whorl at the upper end of the stem and appear in mid-summer.

Range: British Columbia to southern Oregon, from the eastern Cascades to the coast.

Hedgenettle

TALL PENSTEMON
Penstemon procerus
FIGWORT Family

There are many penstemons growing in the Cascades, and often they are difficult to tell apart. However, the penstemon group is easily recognized. The flowers are a double-lipped basket, usually blue in color. The upper lip consists of 2 lobes, the lower lip has three. The word penstemon comes from the Greek for "five stamens". Look for them inside the basket; often they are covered with tiny hairs. One is sterile and bears no pollen. There are about 225 species in North America, mostly in the West. (See also page 144.)

Several penstemons commonly grow in open areas of the forested Cascades. This species is an erect plant, growing up to about 18 inches tall, with half-inch long purple or blue flowers clustered at the top of the stem. Found mainly east of the Cascade crest, it will be seen in mid-summer in dry meadows or on timbered slopes from mid-elevations up to timberline.

Rock penstemon *(P. rupicola)* is a much smaller plant, growing only 3 to 6 inches tall. Its leaves are thick and leathery, only about half an inch long, and rise from woody bases. The flowers often hide them, being over an inch long and a bright rose, pink, or lavender color. This penstemon grows in clumps and may color rocky cliffs in the mountains up to timberline. It is especially vivid in the black lava bordering Fish Lake in the Willamette National Forest, and may be seen along the trail up Garfield Peak in Crater Lake National Park.

Woodland penstemon *(P. nemorosus),* also called turtle-head, is a much larger species, growing 1 to 3 feet tall. Occurring in rocky areas, the plant has one or several erect stems. Its large, coarsely-toothed leaves may be nearly 3 inches long. The flowers are a rose color and may be over one inch long. Since they often grow on rocky outcrops, their large showy blossoms frequently are in the foreground of some beautiful mountain scenery. Woodland penstemon occurs from Washington south to northwestern California.

Range: Mountains of southern Alaska to eastern Washington and Oregon; also the northern Rocky Mountains.

Tall Penstemon

Woodland Penstemon

RED ELDERBERRY
Sambucus racemosa
HONEYSUCKLE Family

This shrub, which bears clusters of white flowers early each summer, may be better known by its fruit than its flowers. By late summer the flowers have matured into bright red berries, conspicuous along the roads of both the coastal mountains and the Cascades. This elderberry may grow as tall as 20 feet. The blue elderberry *(S. cerulea)* grows at low elevations in the Cascades, and throughout the valleys of western Oregon and Washington. Where they both occur, they are easy to distinguish. The blue elderberry has its flowers and fruits in flat-topped clusters, while those of the red elderberry are in pyramid-shaped clusters.

The generic name comes from the Greek word *sambuke,* meaning a musical instrument, parts of which were made from the elder. The pithy stalks are frequently cut to make school children's whistles. In fact, the Indians of California called it "the tree of music". They cut branches from the trees in the spring, then dried them with the leaves on. After the branches dried, holes were bored into them, producing a flute-like whistle. The straight branches were also used for arrows.

Range: Southern Alaska south to central California, from the Cascades to the coast.

Red Elderberry Fruit

SITKA VALERIAN
Valeriana sitchensis
VALERIAN Family

Forming masses of white over alpine meadows and cool forest edges throughout the Cascades, Sitka valerian grows from moderate elevations to timberline, and is very common in the Bird Creek Meadows area of Mt. Adams. The tiny flowers are borne in a cluster at the tip of each stem, which may be 3 feet tall. The extremely fragrant flowers bloom nearly anytime during the short montane summer, when they lend their brightness to the blue of the lupines and reds of the paintbrushes so abundant in mountain areas. The generic name comes from the Latin *valere,* meaning to be strong, and refers to the medicinal value of some members of this genus. The crushed leaves and roots have a strong medicinal odor, although the flowers are sweet-scented.

Range: Mountains of southern Alaska and the Yukon south to northern California and western Montana.

Sitka Valerian

PEARLY EVERLASTING
Anaphalis margaritacea
COMPOSITE Family

The white blossoms of this plant are aptly described by the species name, which means pearly. They are borne atop a 1 to 2 foot tall stem and adorn roadsides and dry waste areas from moderate elevations to timberline. This plant resembles the edelweiss of the European alps, to which it is related. The stems and lower leaf surfaces are covered by white, woolly hairs, giving a silvery appearance to the whole plant. If picked when mature, the flowers do not wilt, but keep their shape indefinitely, and are often used for dried floral arrangements.

The Composite Family is one of the largest families of flowering plants. Each "flower" is composed of many separate flowers clustered into a tight head, giving the non-botanist the impression only one flower is present. These separate flowers are of two types: flat, strap-shaped ones (for instance, those in a dandelion) and tubular ones. The sunflower has both types, each ray being a strap-shaped flower and the center being made up of tubular flowers. The floral head of *Anaphalis* is composed of tubular flowers, surrounded by numerous white, papery bracts.

Range: Western North America and eastern Asia.

WOOLLY YELLOW DAISY
Eriophyllum lanatum
COMPOSITE Family

These bright golden floral heads are carried on such weak stems they may appear to be prostrate. The plant is 4 to 24 inches tall, with finely divided leaves that form a loose mat at the base of the stems and are a dull green or olive color. The stems and leaves are covered with thick, woolly hairs, a characteristic that gave the plant its common name. Both the genus and species names also mean woolly. This is one of the plants whose seeds were collected by the Scottish explorer David Douglas and sent to England. There it has become a common garden flower. In the Northwest, it may be found from lowland valleys to moderate elevations in the mountains.

Range: British Columbia south to California, east to the northern Rocky Mountains.

Woolly Yellow Daisy

YARROW
Achillea millefolium
COMPOSITE Family

Growing at different elevations, this plant has developed into distinct genetic strains. In the lowlands it may reach 4 feet in height, being common along dry roadsides and in open meadows. Forced to curtail its vegetative growth by the short summers above timberline, it grows only 4 or 5 inches tall there. The leaves of the yarrow are finely dissected, often being mistaken for fern leaves, and have a strong odor when crushed. The white floral heads are composed of both disk and ray flowers that bloom from June to August, depending on the elevation. The name *Achillea* refers to the plant that the legendary Achilles used to treat the wounds of his soldiers.

Range: Widespread throughout North America.

Yarrow

BROAD-LEAF ARNICA
Arnica latifolia
COMPOSITE Family

The arnicas may be mistaken for groundsels (see page 88) because both have yellow, sunflower-like floral heads. However, the stem leaves of the arnica are opposite each other, while groundsel leaves are alternate on the stem. A large genus, about 15 species occur in the Northwest.

There are several arnicas in the Cascades. *Arnica latifolia* is one of the most common. It grows up to 2 feet tall and its yellow floral heads may be two inches across. Two or four pairs of leaves grow on each stem. These leaves are oval and coarsely-toothed, only the lower ones having short stems, the others being sessile. Heart-leaved arnica *(A. cordifolia)* is about the same size and also has two to four pairs of stem leaves per plant. Most of the large, heart-shaped leaves are stemmed. Basal leaves are present when this arnica flowers (in broad-leaf arnica the basal leaves are not present at flowering time). *Arnica mollis* is another sparsely-leaved type. Growing 1 or 2 feet tall, its leaves and stems are covered with soft, whitish hairs.

Two other mountain arnicas have from five to twelve pairs of leaves per stem. Long-leaved arnica *(A. longifolia)* is a tufted plant, growing up to 3 feet tall, with smooth leaves that may be 5 inches long. Clumps of long-leaved arnica resemble a low bush with yellow flowers. Clasping leaved arnica *(A. amplexi-caulis)* has sessile, toothed leaves. Its upper leaves tightly clasp the stem.

A drug from the European members of this genus was used in a salve for cuts and was once found in most American medicine chests. The drug was found mainly in the flowers and rootstocks.

Range: Alaska south in the mountains to California and in the northern Rocky Mountains.

Broad-leaf Arnica

ARROWLEAF GROUNDSEL
Senecio triangularis
COMPOSITE Family

The *Senecio* is one of the largest of all known genera, with more than 1,000 species. They all have alternate leaves and small yellow or orange flower heads, with a single row of equal-sized bracts beneath each head. The name *Senecio* comes from the same word as senile and refers to the downy, white hairs on the seed heads, which are supposed to look like an old man's hair.

This *Senecio* is identified by simple, triangular leaves and grows 1 to 3 feet high. It is crowned with numerous small yellow flower heads, thus sprinkling open woods and mountain meadows with golden color. Leaves are found along the entire length of the stem. Another common groundsel *(S. integerrimus)* is similar, but it has a cluster of basal leaves, and the leaves on its stem are progressively smaller, the uppermost leaf being the smallest. In addition, this plant is covered by cob-web like hairs when it is young. Both these groundsels occur in dry or moist open areas, from moderate elevations up to timberline.

Range: Widespread in the mountains of western North America.

Arrowleaf Groundsel

ROSY EVERLASTING
Antennaria rosea
COMPOSITE Family

Also called rosy pussytoes. The everlastings are low, tufted plants. They all have clusters of basal leaves, with alternately arranged stem leaves. These leaves are covered with matted, white hairs, giving the entire plant a soft, fuzzy appearance. The flowers are bunched at the tip of the stems. In this everlasting, the outer bracts beneath each floral head are reddish in color. It grows between 4 and 15 inches tall, although the dry areas it inhabits normally restrict its growth to about 8 inches or less. Look for this *Antennaria* in the bright sunshine of open meadows or rocky areas, where it might be found almost hidden among the dried leaves of native grasses. An *Antennaria* found above timberline is discussed on page 149.

The name everlasting comes from the fact that when this plant is picked it will retain its shape and color almost indefinitely. Thus, it is often found in floral decorations and displays, even though it is not a particularly colorful plant itself.

Range: Widespread in western North America.

Rosy Everlasting

LARGE PURPLE FLEABANE
Erigeron speciosus
COMPOSITE Family

Sometimes called our largest and most showy fleabane, large purple fleabane is common in dry meadows at moderate elevations, especially on the east side of the Cascades. It may grow two feet in height and has leaves the entire length of the stem. Sometimes it forms large clumps in open areas and is then especially conspicuous. The ray flowers are purple, the center disk flowers are yellow. The entire head may be nearly two inches across under favorable conditions, but usually the floral head is only about one inch across. It blooms from May to September.

For a general discussion of fleabanes and asters, see page 147.

Range: Widespread in the mountains of western North America.

Large Purple Fleabane

SKUNK CABBAGE
Lysichitum americanum
ARUM Family

The bright, yellow, hood-shaped sheath (botanically called a spathe) surrounding the skunk cabbage flower stalk is the signal of spring throughout the western states. In mountainous areas it pushes through boggy soils as soon as the snow melts, and can be found at moderate and low elevations mainly on the western side of the Cascades. The flowers are crowded on the tip of the one-foot high floral stalk, which soon grows above its protecting spathe. By late summer only the large cabbage-like leaves remain. When crushed, the leaves and stems produce a skunk-like odor, hence the name skunk cabbage. The genus name *Lysichitum* is from two Greek words, *lysis* meaning loose and *chiton* meaning tunic, and refers to the spathe that wraps loosely around the floral stalk.

The entire plant—leaves, roots, and fruit—are eaten by bears, but the roots are the favored part. Bear and elk will search entire swamps to dig up this delicacy. Many of the Northwestern Indians also sought the roots, baking them to get rid of the hot, peppery taste of the raw material. Skunk cabbage roots were the mainstay of many tribes in the spring when winter food supplies were low.

Range: From Alaska south to central California, east to the northern Rocky Mountains.

Skunk Cabbage

WHITE HELLEBORE
Veratrum californicum
LILY Family

This tall, coarse-leaved plant grows 3 to 4 feet tall in moist mountain meadows, creek bottoms, and lowlands and is crowned by a conspicuous plume of white flowers. It is often accompanied by its cousin false hellebore, *V. viride* (this species name meaning green), which has green flowers instead of white. False hellebore is a more northern species, being found across Canada.

The roots of both hellebores can be very poisonous. False hellebore roots contain alkaloids that slow heartbeat and lower the blood pressure. Indians used them medicinally for these purposes and probably taught this use to the early settlers. However, large doses can be fatal. False hellebore roots have also been used as an insecticide. They are ground or pounded into a powder and sprinkled on garden plants to rid them of worms and insects. The Spaniards in California are said to have made a poison from an extract of white hellebore roots. After fermenting, the juice was put on arrow-

heads. The Spaniards believed that animals were more tender after being shot with a hellebore-poisoned arrow. Both hellebores are considered to be poisonous to livestock and some animals are lost in the spring when they eat the fresh young shoots. However, after the plant is mature and withers, the stem and leaves seem quite harmless.

Range: Washington south through California, east to the Rocky Mountains and south into Mexico.

White Hellebore

COMMON CAMAS
Camassia quamash
LILY Family

The flowers of the common camas have three deep blue sepals and three deep blue petals that look so alike the average observer assumes they have six petals. Sepals and petals are not arranged equally: five are erect or horizontal while one turns downward. Growing 6 to 24 inches tall, the camas has grass-like leaves.

Common in the subalpine meadows of the Cascades, camas was one of the most important of all native plants to the Indians. Tribes cherished the onion-like root and guarded the tribal camas fields from rivals. After the seeds were ripe, bulbs were harvested and baked or roasted for at least 24 hours in a deep hole lined with stones heated in a fire. If not eaten immediately, the blacked outer covering was stripped off and the interior was pressed into a flat cake and hung to dry before storing. The bulb was also dug by the early pioneers and saved many from starvation. In California, settlers made pies from the camas bulb. After stewing, the bulbs took on the consistency of pumpkin.

Care was always taken when digging the camas, however, since the poisonous death-camas *(Zigadenus)* often grows with the edible camas. When flowering they are easily distinguished: the common camas has blue flowers while the death camas has pale greenish-white flowers. However, after the flowering season they look very much alike because death-camas is also 1 to 2 feet tall and has grass-like leaves.

Range: British Columbia south through the Coast Range and Cascades to California, east to the northern Rocky Mountains.

Common Camas

TOFIELDIA
Tofieldia glutinosa
LILY Family

Also called false or Scottish asphodel. Blooming in June and July, tofieldia grows 4 to 20 inches tall and has cream-colored flowers borne in terminal clusters. The unbranching stems rise from a short, basal rootstalk and have grass-like leaves that are slightly sticky to the touch—glutinosa means sticky. Tofieldia may be found in wet meadows and along streambanks at moderate elevations in the mountains in the company of the bog orchid, ladies' tresses, common camas, and death-camas, which it closely resembles.

Range: Alaska to Newfoundland, south in the mountains to California, Wyoming, and North Carolina.

Tofieldia

WHITE BOG ORCHID
Habenaria dilatata
ORCHID Family

These tapering spikes of white flowers are conspicuous along wet roadsides and meadows at moderate elevations throughout the Cascades. They stand about one foot tall, so the flowers grow above most of the grasses and sedges sharing the moist spots where this orchid occurs. This species is often accompanied by the less showy, somewhat shorter green bog orchid *(H. saccata).* Both flower during June, July, and August, depending on the elevation.

There are about 500 species of *Habenaria* in temperate and tropical regions. The flowers of most of those found in the mountains of the Northwest are rather small, but looking at them closely, one can see the beautiful structure of the well-known, larger tropical orchids. The genus name is from the Latin word meaning reins or slender strap and refers to the narrow lip found on many species of the genus.

Range: Widespread across northern North America and in the western mountains.

White Bog Orchid (left), Green Bog Orchid (right)

LADIES' TRESSES
Spiranthes romanzoffiana
ORCHID Family

Resembling finely braided hair, these white flowers form a spiral twist atop a ½ to 2 foot tall stem. Indeed, the name *Spiranthes* refers to this trait, being derived from the Greek words *speira* (meaning coil) and *anthos* (meaning flower). Ladies' tresses is a late bloomer, even by alpine standards, appearing abundantly in August along lakeshores, streams, and other wet areas. Linear, grass-like leaves grow from the lower portion of the stem and are usually hidden amid the grasses and sedges abounding where ladies' tresses grows. There are over 100 species of *Spiranthes* growing throughout the world; however, this is the only one in the Northwest.

Range: Widespread across western and northern North America.

Ladies' Tresses

SPRING BEAUTY
Claytonia lanceolata
PURSLANE Family

This dainty flower welcomes spring in April and May at lower elevations, while it still may be found high on the north slopes of our taller peaks during mid-August. It may be found in sagebrush foothills or high alpine slopes, wherever the ground is moist in the spring.

It consists of a short stem—about 3 inches tall—with a single pair of opposite stem leaves, and about 3 to 10 pale pinkish flowers.

There are about 10 species of *Claytonia* in North America, most of them being found in mountainous areas or in the Arctic regions. The plant was named for a botanist who collected specimens mainly from the east coast, John Clayton (1685-1773). The stems and leaves of many *Claytonia* have been used as food. The round basal portion of this plant, relished by the Indians, has a taste similar to radishes when eaten raw. When cooked, it tastes somewhat like a baked potato.

Range: Widespread in the mountains of the western states.

YELLOW POND LILY
Nuphar polysepalum
WATER LILY Family

The large, circular leaves of this plant may be found floating on the surface of quiet ponds and marshes, attached by a long stem to the thick rootstock anchored in the mud below. The Indians called this plant wokas. Many Indian tribes, notably the Klamath Indians, depended heavily on the wokas for food. They annually trekked to the Klamath Marsh to await the ripening of the seeds. They danced and held ceremonies until the seeds were ripe, and then gathered the wokas in huge hand-made sacks. The women ground most of the seeds to powder and flour; some were roasted and eaten like popcorn.

Range: Alaska to California, east through the northern Rocky Mountains.

Yellow Pond Lily

COLUMBINE
Aquilegia formosa
BUTTERCUP Family

The showy, scarlet flowers of this common wildflower cannot be mistaken for any other. They are often cultivated and planted in gardens where they are established easily by seed. Some species of columbine in the Rocky Mountains are blue—the state flower of Colorado is a blue columbine —while some of those in the Southwest are yellow. There are over 70 species of columbine occurring in the Northern Hemisphere; of these, four are found in the Northwest. The only other columbine in the Cascades is *A. flavescens,* which is yellow instead of red, and not nearly as common.

Growing 1½ to 3 feet tall, *A. formosa* is generally found in moist, shaded areas. The brightly colored flowers usually rise from a dense clump of basal leaves, divided into threes. According to some, the spurred petals of the flower resemble an eagle's claw—indeed the genus name is derived from the word *aquila,* which means eagle.

Range: Mostly along the coast and in the mountains from Alaska to Baja California; also in the northern Rockies.

Columbine

FALSE BUGBANE
Trautvetteria caroliniensis
BUTTERCUP Family

This beautiful plant of moist mountain areas is topped with bright white flower clusters. It owes its spectacular appearance not to floral petals, but stamens. In fact, it has no petals whatsoever. Each small flower has an abundant number of white stamens, giving the floral balls a fuzzy appearance. Standing 2 or 3 feet tall, the plant has large (2 to 6 inches wide) maple-like leaves. False bugbane may be found in marshes, along shaded streambanks, and around mountain lakes.

Range: Moderate elevations in the mountains of the western United States and British Columbia.

False Bugbane

MONKSHOOD
Aconitum columbianum
BUTTERCUP Family

This beautiful blue flower may be found in moist woods and subalpine meadows, where it flowers from late June to early August, depending on elevation. The genus name comes from the ancient Greek word for the plant. The common name is derived from the hood-shaped sepal of the flower, said to look like the helmet worn by medieval monks. The stem is 2 to 4 feet tall and supports a long, loose cluster of flowers, each of which may be an inch long. The leaves, arranged alternately on the stem, are palmately veined and deeply lobed. The larger leaves at the base of the plant may be nearly 4 inches wide; those at the upper part of the stem are smaller. Although there are from 50 to 100 species of monkshood in the North Temperate Zone of North America, Europe, and Asia, this is the only species found in the Northwest.

The entire plant is poisonous, containing the alkaloids aconitine and aconine. The root, generally unpalatable to livestock, is the most potent part. The drug aconite, used as a sedative, is derived from a European monkshood.

Range: Widespread in the mountains of western North America, east to the Black Hills.

GRASS-OF-PARNASSUS
Parnassia fimbriata
SAXIFRAGE Family

Five creamy-white petals, fringed at each side, identify the flowers of this plant. The single flower is borne on a stem about a foot tall with a single small stem leaf and several smooth, heart-shaped basal leaves. It is common in marshy areas, such as the shores of Trillium Lake on the south slope of Mt. Hood, around Todd Lake in the Three Sisters, and other wet areas. It may be found from moderate elevations in the mountains up to higher elevations. The genus name *Parnassia* is derived from a mountain in Greece that was well-known in ancient mythology. Sacred to Apollo, it was the home of the Muses, the nine goddesses of song and poetry.

Range: Widespread in the mountains of the western United States.

Grass-of-Parnassus

MOUNTAIN SPIREA
Spiraea densiflora
ROSE Family

Found from moderate elevations to timberline meadows, this small shrub has flat-topped clusters of tiny pink flowers. The shrubs may be about 3 feet tall and are found in moist meadows, along streams, and around lakes.

Often accompanying it is the steeple-bush, *Spiraea douglasii*. Steeple-bush, however, has pyramid-shaped clusters of pink flowers and may grow nearly 6 feet tall. It is not confined to alpine regions, and also grows in wet areas in the lowland valleys and along the coast. In some areas it is widely cultivated and used in yards and gardens.

The genus name is from the Greek word *speira,* meaning "something wrapped in a coil." These beautiful flowers have long been used to make floral wreaths, and perhaps this is how the name originated. These shrubs also have a functional value: their dense foliage provides shelter for many small animals and birds, such as rabbits, grouse, quail, and other forest inhabitants.

Range: Common in the mountains of northwestern North America.

Mountain Spirea

DEVIL'S CLUB
Oplopanax horridum
GINSENG Family

Growing abundantly in moist, deep soil, devil's club is conspicuous wherever it is found. A robust plant with stems that may be nearly an inch thick, devil's club grows 3 to 12 feet tall. Long yellow spines arm the stems and branches. Even the large, maple-like leaves have spines projecting from their undersides. Anyone attempting to walk through a thicket of devil's club will remember these spines because they tear at both clothing and skin. A shrubby, luxurious plant, devil's club is common along streams and in moist woodlands at lower elevations. During June, white or pale green flowers appear in open, branched clusters. By August, these are replaced with bright red berries.

Range: Alaska south along the coast and on the western side of the Cascades to southern Oregon; also in the northern Rocky Mountains.

Devil's Club

GRAY'S LOVAGE
Ligusticum grayi
PARSLEY Family

Common in wet meadows and open places within Lassen Volcanic National Park, in Eden Park on the north slope of Mt. Hood, at Sunshine Shelter in the Willamette National Forest, and many other moist spots in the Cascades, this plant resembles the lowland Queen Anne's lace. Growing from a very large, aromatic root, it stands about 2 to 3 feet high and is characterized by large, lace-like leaves and a round-topped cluster of white flowers, which may be 2 to 5 inches across. This flower cluster is typical of the parsley family and is called an umbel— all the stems originate from the same point like the ribs of an umbrella. This is an extremely large family and can always be recognized by the parsley-like head of flowers. Many plants of economic value belong to this family: celery, parsnip, dill, and caraway are only a few.

Range: Mountainous areas of the Pacific states.

Gray's Lovage

COW PARSNIP
Heracleum lanatum
PARSLEY Family

The generic name is derived from the name Hercules and denotes the large proportions of this plant, which may grow up to 8 feet tall, while the species name refers to the hairy covering found over most of this plant.

The stout-stemmed plant has large leaves (divided into three parts), that may be nearly 10 inches wide. The small, white flowers are in large, flat-topped clusters that are usually from 4 to 10 inches across.

The huge stem is edible. It may be cut before the flowers open and, with the outer covering peeled off, sliced and prepared much like rhubarb. It may also be eaten raw: the stems are sliced into very thin pieces and used as salad greens. The Pacific Indians from Alaska to California used the tender young leaves for food. It is also said that they took the basal portion of the plant, burned it, and used the ashes for salt. In addition, some Indians used a preparation made from the mashed root to alleviate a sore throat. After soaking the root in water, the resulting solution was gargled. The plant is readily eaten by wild and domestic animals alike, and is rare in areas grazed by cattle.

About 60 species of *Heracleum* grow in the world. This is the only one in the Northwest.

Range: Most of North America, Siberia, and the Kurile Islands.

Cow Parsnip

RED-OSIER DOGWOOD
Cornus stolonifera
var. *occidentalis*
DOGWOOD Family

This shrub or small tree—which may reach 15 feet in height—differs from the more spectacular flowering Pacific dogwood. (See page 43). It has flat-topped cymes of small white flowers rather than showy bracts. Also, the berries are white instead of red like those of the bunchberry and the Pacific dogwood. However, this species is well-known for its bright red bark, especially conspicuous in the winter, and it is often planted in gardens to add color when the leaves have fallen from other shrubs.

Found along streams and pond margins from moderate elevations to timberline, the red-osier dogwood is common throughout the Cascades. *Range:* Over most of North America. Some authorities say the eastern plant is a different species than the western variety; however, the transition of features from east to west is so gradual that other authorities believe they are the same.

Red-osier Dogwood

ALPINE SHOOTING STAR
Dodecatheon alpinum
PRIMROSE Family

Also known as bird-bill. This beautiful, purple flower, about an inch long, is easily recognized by its four reflexed petals. The leaves are all basal, forming a rosette, and are from 2 to 6 inches long, the flowers being elevated nearly a foot above them. It is most often found in wet meadows near or above timberline, in the company of the white marsh marigold, elephanthead, fanleaf cinquefoil, and subalpine buttercup.

Slightly taller and more robust, the rose-colored Jeffrey shooting star *(D. jeffreyi)* may grow nearly a foot and a half high and has leaves up to 12 inches long. It is most often found in wet woodland openings surrounded by silver fir or mountain hemlock. In the northern Oregon Cascades both of these shooting stars may be found; however, the alpine shooting star is the more common in the southern Cascades, especially around Crater Lake and Lassen Peak.

Range: Oregon Cascades south through the Sierra Nevada, east to the southern Rocky Mountains.

Alpine Shooting Star

COMMON GENTIAN
Gentiana sceptrum
GENTIAN Family

While this gentian may be called common, this does not mean the flower is not spectacular. It grows nearly 3 feet tall in the grassy sod of boggy areas such as Summit Meadows and Little Crater Lake on the south slopes of Mt. Hood. The deep blue flowers are present only as unopened buds most of August. They generally open after Labor Day. This is a large genus and gentians may be found in mountains all over the world. Similar species occur in the American Rockies, the Swiss Alps, the Asian Himalayas, and the Andes of South America. Some 300 species occur in temperate and Arctic regions of the world, with about 15 recorded in the Northwest.

The pleated gentian *(Gentiana calycosa)* is another common alpine species and grows in most of the mountains in the Pacific Northwest and in the northern Rocky Mountains. Its flowers are also deep blue, but the plants are smaller, growing to about 1 foot tall, and only one flower occurs on each stem. Its flowers are marked by yellowish dots and have conspicuous teeth in the notches between the petal lobes. *Gentiana newberryi* is found in the high Cascades in southern Oregon and the Sierra Nevada in California. It is a dwarf plant, barely growing 4 inches tall. It may be found sparingly in the Three Sisters area.

Range: Southwestern British Columbia south through western Washington and Oregon to northern California.

Common Gentian

TALL LUNGWORT
Mertensia paniculata
BORAGE Family

Also called bluebells. The pendant blue flowers easily identify this shrub, which grows about 3 to 4 feet high. When the buds first appear, they are pink, as are the flowers when they first open. However, the tubular, bell-shaped flowers gradually turn a rich blue color. The drooping branches have alternate leaves, which are covered with tiny hairs, giving them a bluish tinge. This off-green color will help identify the plant from a distance. Tall lungwort can be very plentiful along creek bottoms, lake shores, and moist open spots from the foothills to higher elevations. It is especially common around Trillium Lake and at Hood River Meadows on Mt. Hood.

Range: Alaska south through the Cascades to southern Oregon; also the Olympic Mountains; east to Quebec and Iowa.

Tall Lungwort

113

COMMON MONKEYFLOWER
Mimulus guttatus
FIGWORT Family

These yellow blossoms, which resemble a cultivated snapdragon, may be found along trickles of water throughout the Cascades. The yellow throat is generally dotted with ·small, red flecks. Being so widespread, the plant varies in general appearance with elevation and local climatic conditions. At medium elevations it may grow nearly 2 feet tall, but barely reach 3 inches above timberline. The common name monkeyflower refers to the funny-face mask that some brightly-colored members of this genus resemble. The genus name is from the diminutive of the Latin *mimus,* meaning a mimic actor.

There are several other common species of monkeyflower occurring in the Pacific Northwest and in northern California. The primrose monkeyflower *(Mimulus primuloides)* has a very tiny, single, yellow flower growing from the top of a slender 2 to 4 inch stem. Often associated with it is the yellow-flowered muskplant monkeyflower *(M. moschatus),* which grows along the ground and usually is only about 6 inches tall. Its leaves and stems are covered with tiny white hairs, making it slimy to touch when wet.

Monkeyflowers also come in various shades of purple. The Lewis monkeyflower *(M. lewisii)* is found in alpine streams and springs, sometimes above timberline, and is a taller, more robust plant than the other species mentioned here. It grows in clumps up to 2 feet tall and varies in color from pale lavender to pink. It was named after Captain Meriwether Lewis of the Lewis and Clark Expedition in the Northwest in 1804-1806. The only member of this group discussed here that is found on drier soils is the dwarf monkeyflower, *Mimulus nanus.* It consists of short, branched stems 1 to 5 inches tall, growing best where it is partly shaded. It appears as patches of reddish-purple along the roadside around Bend, Oregon, and in the pumice areas of Crater Lake National Park.

Range: Widespread in the western states and Canada. Has been introduced into Europe.

Common Monkeyflower

Lewis Monkeyflower

ELEPHANTHEAD
Pedicularis groenlandica
FIGWORT Family

Also called fernleaf. The tall spires of this plant protrude above swampy areas and along streams from moderate to high elevations throughout the Cascades, usually in the company of monkeyflower, camas, and the slender bog orchid. The plant stands from 8 to 24 inches high, and the stems carry fern-like leaves. Each flower has a long, upward curving petal and two lateral petals. It takes little imagination to see an elephant's head with the curved petal as the trunk and the two lateral petals as large flapping ears. The flowers are not easily mistaken for any other. The flowers are a dull red or purple and appear in July and August. The name *Pedicularis* means louse in Latin—legend says that cattle eating these plants become infected with lice. The species name indicates this plant occurs in Greenland.

Closely resembling elephanthead but being much smaller (6 to 12 inches tall), *P. attolens* is found frequently in Cascade Mountain meadows south of McKenzie Pass. Like elephanthead, its flowers are a reddish-purple—it resembles a miniature of *P. groenlandica* and is often called little elephanthead. It is especially abundant around the shoreline of Todd Lake in the Three Sisters area.

A close relative, wood betony or bracted pedicularis *(Pedicularis bracteosa)* may be found growing alongside elephanthead. It is also a flower of high alpine elevations, growing in wet areas. The upper lobe of each flower consists of a one-half inch hooded lip. The flowers are usually yellow, but may be pinkish or even a dull green or purple. The plants are 1 to 2 feet tall and have triangular, deeply dissected leaves, which may be 1 to 6 inches long. These leaves turn purple as they age.

Range: Widespread in the mountains of western North America, east across southern Canada to Labrador.

Wood Betony

Elephanthead

COMMON PAINTBRUSH
Castilleja miniata
FIGWORT Family

Also called painted-cup. There are about 200 species of *Castilleja*—nearly 40 of them occur in the Northwest. They are difficult to tell apart and vary in color from yellow to pink, deep red, or vivid magenta. The color is actually due to the ragged bracts below each flower and the flower sepals. These bracts look as if each had been dipped into a paint bucket and produce the beautiful color for which paintbrushes are known. The floral petals themselves are usually small and inconspicuous, being dull yellow or green. They are hidden among the brightly colored bracts. The genus was named for the Spanish botanist Domingo Castillejo.

This is the most common paintbrush in the western states, occurring in each state and province of western North America. It is identified by its smooth, mostly entire leaves (the leaves of most other paintbrushes are lobed). It is a stout plant, growing up to 2 or 3 feet tall, and has a brilliant head of red or scarlet-tipped bracts. The real flowers, tucked between the bracts, are narrow and tubular. In the Cascades this paintbrush occurs at moderate elevations in moist open meadows and along streambanks. The paintbrushes that are more common above timberline are found on page 145.

Range: Widespread in western North America.

Common Paintbrush

TWINBERRY
Lonicera involucrata
HONEYSUCKLE Family

Also called bush honeysuckle and inkberry. The deep-green, glossy leaves make this an extremely striking shrub. Growing 5 to 8 feet high, it has erect, yellow flowers from May to July and, later, black berries surrounded by dark red bracts. Both the flowers and the berries occur in pairs, which explains the common name. Twinberry flourishes in moist woods, along lake margins, and in boggy areas, where it may be hidden by the thick growth of devil's club, willow, spirea, and cow parsnip. It may be found along the coast and up to fairly high elevations in the mountains.

Range: Southwestern Alaska south to northern Mexico, east across North America to Quebec.

Twinberry

CREEK GOLDENROD
Solidago canadensis
COMPOSITE Family

Also called meadow golden-rod. Growing 2 or 3 feet high, this goldenrod may be found along streambanks and other moist situations, where its pyramidal spray of yellow flowers appears in July and August and may continue to bloom through the fall. They forecast cooler weather ahead. Individuals of this group of plants are extremely difficult to tell apart from each other, so it is quite permissible to simply refer to the whole group as "goldenrod."

The yellow flowers of some species once were used to make a yellow dye, lending color to Indian crafts and clothing. The Indians also boiled the leaves to make a preparation to put on cuts and flesh wounds. Indeed, the genus name is derived from the Latin word meaning "to make whole."
Range: Throughout most of North America.

Creek Goldenrod

COLTSFOOT
Petasites frigidus
COMPOSITE Family

One of the earliest spring flowers to bloom, coltsfoot pushes its head through the leaves and duff along stream-banks, in moist woods, and beside roadways. Often the leaf does not appear until after the flower has bloomed. The loose-clustered flower heads are on the top of a thick stem that may be over one foot tall and has scale-like leaves along its entire length. The flowers are pale pink to lavender or white, becoming seeds of the same color. As the flowers wither, a large, palmately-lobed leaf unfolds, umbrella-like, and remains throughout the summer. The leaves may be nearly one foot wide and have soft, woolly hairs on their undersides. The name *Petasites* comes from the ancient Greek word for a broad-brimmed hat, un-doubtedly referring to the wide leaf.

Range: Circumboreal, extending across the northern portions of North America and south through the Cascades westward to the coast.

Coltsfoot

119

AVALANCHE LILY
Erythronium montanum
LILY Family

Also called dogtooth violet, alpine fawn lily. Wherever the snow has melted this lily carpets mountain meadows and forests, its white blossoms dancing in the constant alpine breeze. Its blooming period depends on the local snow conditions and topography—

in Paradise Park on the southwest slopes of Mt. Hood it blooms in early July or as soon as the snow melts. However, it may bloom in late August on the sheltered north slopes of Mt. Hood.

The glacier lily *(E. grandiflorum)* is another timberline flower, blooming alongside melting snowbanks. It occurs in the Washington and Oregon Cascades, the Olympics, and the northern Rocky Mountains. Both plants grow between 3 and 16 inches tall, but can easily be distinguished because the avalanche lily is white, the glacier lily is yellow.

The *Erythronium* bulb was readily eaten by the Indians, who boiled it or dried it for storage. They also used the leaves and ate them raw. The fresh seed pods were boiled and taste much like string beans.

Range: Cascades of Washington and northern Oregon and the Olympics.

Glacier Lily

Avalanche Lily

CAT'S EAR
Calochortus subalpinus
LILY Family

Also called Mariposa lily and sego lily. The name cat's ear reflects the soft, hairy inner surfaces of the three petals that form the cup-shaped flowers. Growing from 3 to 8 inches tall, this *Calochortus* is abundant on the grassy alpine slopes and meadows along the Pacific Crest Trail. It is easily recognized by its three hairy, white petals alternating with three green sepals and the narrow, glossy, green linear leaves. A small purple dot near the base of each sepal distinguishes this cat's ear from the lowland form, *C. tolmiei*, which ranges south into the Sierra Nevada.
Range: Cascades of Washington and Oregon.

Cat's Ear

AMERICAN BISTORT
Polygonum bistortoides
BUCKWHEAT Family

This alpine buckwheat is found in moist meadows along streambanks and mountain slopes at middle and high elevations. The tufts of tiny white flowers sway in the mountain breeze on slender, grass-like stems two or three feet tall. The narrow oblong leaves, mostly basal, are 6 to 12 inches long. They rise from a thick, starchy rootstock, reputedly used in soups and as a vegetable by the Alaskan Eskimos and several Indian tribes of the Rocky Mountains.

Range: Widespread in the mountains of the western states.

American Bistort

NEWBERRY KNOTWEED
Polygonum newberryi
BUCKWHEAT Family

This perennial pushes its way through the rocky soil above timberline as the snow recedes, first appearing as brilliant red shoots. Thick, tuberous roots send up several reddish stems (up to 12 inches long) with fleshy, dull-green leaves. These wither and blow away in the dry mountain winds before the end of the short summer. The greenish flowers are inconspicuous and easily overlooked; however, the plant itself catches the eye because it often dominates pumice and gravel slopes and is very important in holding soil in place. This knotweed may be found on exposed places at high elevations along the entire Cascade Range.

Range: Olympic Mountains; Cascades and northern Sierra Nevada; also central Idaho.

Newberry Knotweed

MOUNTAIN SORREL
Oxyria digyna
BUCKWHEAT Family

Also called alpine sorrel. The only member of this genus, mountain sorrel grows in moist ground, usually in rock scree or crevices above timberline. Look for it when exploring the rocky areas of Broken Top Crater, Mt. Jefferson, Crater Lake, and other high alpine areas. It is small (6 to 12 inches tall), with tiny, greenish flowers, bright red seeds, and kidney-shaped leaves. The plant is more conspicuous when the flat, red fruits are present than when it is in flower. The name *Oxyria* comes from the Greek word *oxys*, meaning sharp, or sour, referring to the strongly acid juice of the plant. Mountain climbers and back-packers find the leaves pleasantly sour and a refreshing change in their diet of freeze-dried food. The leaves can be eaten as salad greens and are used by the Eskimos to prevent scurvy, since it is rich in vitamin C.

Range: Circumpolar, occurring in the northern portions and mountains of North America, Europe, and Asia.

Mountain Sorrel

SULPHUR-FLOWER
Eriogonum umbellatum
BUCKWHEAT Family

Found on the rocky exposures of higher elevations, these bright golden flowers may cover entire slopes with vivid color. However, sulphur-flower is quite variable, and many members of this species have dull yellow or cream-colored blossoms. The flowers are tightly clustered into an umbrella-like head at the tip of a 4 to 12 inch, leafless stem. These stems grow from a woody base and bear small, silvery-green leaves, arranged in whorls. Clumps of sulphur-flower occupy crevices and cracks where one would not expect plants to survive. The thick spatulate or oval leaves huddle close to the ground, where most of the alpine winds will not reach them and are covered with tiny hairs, thought by some to protect them from desiccation.

Several other *Eriogonums* occur on the high slopes of the Cascades. *Eriogonum ovalifolium* also has silver-colored leaves, but they are more oval in shape. A dense head of yellow flowers rises about one foot above the basal leaves. This species grows in the sagebrush desert as well as on alpine slopes. It occurs from British Columbia through the Cascade and Sierra Nevada Mountains to southern California and in the Rocky Mountains. Another common *Eriogonum* found from Harts Pass in Washington south on high alpine peaks to Lassen Peak in California is one dubbed with the common name of "dirty socks" *(E. pyrolaefolium).* One smell of its blossoms will explain the name! It has white flowers and basal, oval leaves. The stems are about 3 to 4 inches tall and grow from a woody base. This eriogonum grows on open, pumice flats and is especially abundant in Broken Top Crater and Jefferson Park.

Range: British Columbia south on the east side of the Cascades to the Sierra Nevada of southern California east to the Rocky Mountains.

Dirty Socks

Sulphur-flower

UMBELLATE PUSSYPAWS
Spraguea umbellata
PURSLANE Family

Flattened against gravelly alpine soil, pussypaws' fleshy leaves radiate out from a thickened taproot that may extend many feet into the soil as an anchor in the unstable mountain slopes. Roots up to 11 feet in length have been measured. The pinkish flowers extend beyond the leaves, stretching out like a cat's paw. This is a mountain-loving plant—look for it along timberline where it may be found in the company of the gnarled whitebark pine and the raucous Clark's nutcracker. Below timberline this plant is often used as an indicator of very sterile soil—it is abundant on the Pumice Desert in Crater Lake National Park and on the pumice flats around Sparks Lake in the Deschutes National Forest.

Range: Widespread in the mountains of the western states.

Umbellate Pussypaws

SANDWORT
Arenaria capillaris
PINK Family

Without the flowers, the tufted needle-like leaves make this plant resemble a tiny pine seedling. The white, five-petaled flowers are borne on thin, erect stems, about 6 inches tall. Sandwort thrives in barren, sandy soil: in fact, *Arenaria* is derived from the Latin word for sand. There are nearly 200 different sandworts occupying a wide range of habitats and geographic locations. Some species inter-grade and hybridize and so they are difficult to distinguish. However, you can recognize the genus by its linear, matted leaves and white, star-shaped flowers.

Range: High mountain areas from Alaska south through Oregon, east to the northern Rockies.

Sandwort

WESTERN PASQUE FLOWER
Anemone occidentalis
BUTTERCUP Family

Only those venturing into the high country when the snows are melting at timberline have the privilege of seeing this beautiful flower, usually blooming at the edge of a retreating snowbank. The waxy-white blossoms are composed of sepals, not petals. When flowering, the plant is only about 5 inches tall; by the time it fruits at the end of the summer, it has grown to nearly 24 inches tall. The stem and finely-divided leaves are covered with short, compact hairs. Some feel that this insulating "fur coat" helps retard the loss of metabolic heat and protects the vulnerable stem and leaves from wind desiccation. By late July and August the fruiting head of silky, greenish tassels has developed. Looking much like a mop head or a hoary, bearded mane, it is often referred to as "old man of the mountain." The species name *occidentalis* means from the west. Anemones are widespread throughout North America; however, this species is found only in western mountains.

Range: Northern British Columbia, south through the Cascades and Olympics; also the Sierra Nevada and the northern Rocky Mountains.

Western Pasque Flower

Western Pasque Flower fruit

WHITE MARSH MARIGOLD
Caltha biflora
BUTTERCUP Family

The bright, waxy-white sepals of these alpine flowers radiate out from a yellow center, like a spot of sunshine. The blossoms are an inch or more across. The round, kidney-shaped leaves are mostly basal and their satiny surface reflects the sun. Less than a foot tall, this marigold is found in the wet alpine woodlands and meadows at higher elevations. It frequently grows in the melt-water of a nearby snowbank or along an alpine stream. Similar, but with elongate, heart-shaped leaves, *Caltha leptosepala,* may also be found in high mountain meadows.

Range: High mountains from Alaska to California, east to the central Rockies.

White Marsh Marigold

SUBALPINE BUTTERCUP
Ranunculus eschscholtzii
BUTTERCUP Family

Flowering in July and August, this small buttercup may be found in wet alpine meadows. Since these plants often grow in small clumps, their glossy yellow petals contrast sharply with the surrounding green sedges and low grasses. This buttercup grows 2 to 10 inches tall, and has deeply cleft leaves, the lower ones long-petioled, the stem leaves sessile.

Observations of alpine butter-cups in the Rocky Mountains show that they often begin growing before the snowbank under which they spent the winter has entirely melted. A snowbank can actually be a blessing to a small alpine plant—it protects from the severe winter winds and insulates from below zero temperatures. In actuality, the buttercup is a "fair-weather" bloomer in the high country. Only during the warm months of summer does the buttercup make its appear-ance. Indeed, such timing is one of the most valuable adaptations alpine plants possess.

Range: Moist alpine and subalpine areas of the western states.

Subalpine Buttercup

STONECROP
Sedum divergens
STONECROP Family

These rock-loving plants have thick succulent leaves adapted for water storage. Many suppose that the stonecrop can live and thrive without much water; however, like the cacti of the American Southwest, the stonecrop does need moisture and grows best during the seasons when water is available. It is more correct to say stonecrop requires well-drained situations, and this is why it thrives in rocky areas. During dry periods, it uses the water stored in its leaves. When the moisture is expended, the plant may lie dormant for long periods of time until water is again available. In this species the thick, nearly circular leaves are mostly opposite each other on its 2 to 6 inch stem. Most of the leaves are in compact, basal rosettes. Look for it on alpine and sub-alpine slopes and rocky ledges.

Range: Olympic and Cascade Mountains of Washington and northern Oregon.

Stonecrop

TOLMIE SAXIFRAGE
Saxifraga tolmiei
SAXIFRAGE Family

The white flowers and small, thickened leaves of this saxifrage form a low-lying mat over the rocky areas above timberline, particularly along the northern section of the Timberline Trail around Mt. Hood, and the rocky areas along the Summit Trail on Mt. Shasta, and the Pacific Crest Trail. The succulent nature of the leaves allows storage of snow melt-water that can be used later in the summer when the barren rocky outcrops have been drained of moisture. The flowers themselves are on erect 2 to 4 inch stems and look dainty, being less than one-half inch wide with dark purple-tipped stamens. Their habitat is explained by the generic name, which means breaker of rocks. These flowers seem to thrive in otherwise barren, rocky situations. The specific name honors a pioneer surgeon, botanist, and mountaineer W. F. Tolmie.

Range: Alaska south through the Cascades to the central Sierra Nevada, east in the high mountains to Montana and Idaho.

Tolmie Saxifrage

FANLEAF CINQUEFOIL
Potentilla flabellifolia
ROSE Family

Also called five-finger. Over 30 species of *Potentilla* occur in the Northwest, and several of these frequent the mountains. The common name cinquefoil originates from the words meaning "five" and "leaf" and refers to those species with five leaflets. Superficially resembling a yellow buttercup, individual cinquefoils may be difficult to tell apart. However, they are easy to distinguish from the buttercups. All have five bright-yellow petals (as do the buttercups), alternating with five green sepals. Five shorter green bracts alternate with the sepals and this arrangement will help you distinguish the group from the buttercups. (See pages 68 and 133.)

Fanleaf cinquefoil is one of the most common of the cinquefoils found in high elevation alpine meadows and grows about 12 inches tall. The leaves remind one of a strawberry plant, the wedge-shaped leaflets being in threes. At Paradise Park on Mt. Hood it blooms in early July, when this mountain meadow is just beginning to blossom with paintbrushes, lupines, and wild buckwheats. It is common in the wet alpine meadows along the Pacific Crest Trail.

Another cinquefoil common in some high elevation areas is the woody-stemmed shrubby cinquefoil *(P. fruticosa)*. It is a spreading, bushy shrub, growing up to 4 feet tall.

Range: Mountains of British Columbia, south through the Cascades to northern California; east in the mountains to Idaho, Montana, and Alberta.

Fanleaf Cinquefoil

PARTRIDGE FOOT
Luetkea pectinata
ROSE Family

Also called Alaska spirea. A low-growing, spirea-like plant less than a foot tall, this dainty alpine perennial is plentiful in open areas around timberline throughout the Cascades, forming a white halo above its mats of green, finely divided leaves. The plant grows over a wide area where conditions are favorable and makes an excellent ground cover. Often it is found in the partial shade formed by wind-pruned whitebark pine, alternating with clumps of dwarf juniper. It grows best along rocky springs but is found also along exposed ridges. Look for it on the pumice slopes of Mt. St. Helens near timberline, and along the slopes of Squaw Valley on Mt. Shasta. Partridge foot spreads easily with small cuttings and divisions taking root. There is only one species in this genus, which was named for the Russian Count F. P. Luetke, an Arctic explorer. The name partridge foot comes from the shape of the leaves.

Range: Widespread in the northern mountains of western North America.

Partridge Foot

LOW MOUNTAIN LUPINE
Lupinus lepidus
PEA Family

There are more than 40 species of lupine growing in the Northwest. One might attempt to learn a few of the easily recognized ones, lumping the rest under the general name "lupine". Lupines as a group are recognized by their leaflets, which radiate out from the tip of a petiole like the fingers of a hand. The number of leaflets varies with the different species. (Also see page 72.) This is probably the most typical of all the lupines growing at timberline and above and has been known previously as *Lupinus Lyallii*. It seems to thrive on the open pumice slopes around Crater Lake, in the Three Sisters area, and the timberline regions around Mt. Hood and Mt. Jefferson. Look for it along open dry stretches and beneath lodgepole pine forests along the Pacific Crest

Trail. It is easily recognized because of its silvery-green leaves and low growth form. The whole plant may not rise more than a few inches off the ground. The flowers are clustered at the tip of a leafless, 2 to 6 inch long, decumbent stem. The basal leaves are composed of 5 or 7 oblong leaflets, which fold at night. The deep blue to lavender-colored flowers contrast with the otherwise barren surroundings.

Range: Widespread in the high mountains of north-western North America.

Low Mountain Lupine

FEW-FRUITED DESERT PARSLEY
Lomatium martindalei
PARSLEY Family

This little parsley abounds on open pumice soil and dry slopes near timberline. The flowers may be white or yellow and the leaves, mostly basal, are finely dissected. Although the flowering stalk extends only 4 or 5 inches above the ground, the fleshy taproot may be more than one foot long. *All Lomatiums* have thick, fleshy roots and many were used by the Indians for food, either roasted or raw.

The journals of Lewis and Clark tell of purchasing *Lomatium* roots as food for the group.

In many ways alpine areas are very much like deserts—there is a constant, drying wind, the porous soil does not hold moisture, the relative humidity is very low, the growing season is short, and temperatures fluctuate widely. Therefore, plants growing in both areas often have many characteristics in common: a large root system to sustain the plant through winter (or drought), small stature (plants low to the ground avoid much of the drying winds), and slow growth because of the short growing season. Many desert parsleys also occur in the hot desert of the Southwest and the cold sagebrush desert of the Great Basin states.

Range: Mountainous areas from British Columbia south through Oregon.

Few-fruited Desert Parsley

MOUNTAIN HEATHER
Phyllodoce empetriformis
HEATH Family

Also called heather and pink heather. This is a mat-forming species, nestling in rocky outcrops beneath towering peaks. A sprawling, woody shrub, it usually is less than 20 inches high. Its evergreen needle-like leaves and pink, urn-shaped flowers contrast sharply with the dull gray of nearby talus slopes. It may be the only plant covering large alpine areas. Its near cousin may also be found in the rocky outcrops of timberline—the yellow heather, *P. glanduliflora.* This heather is similar in appearance, also having short, needle-like, evergreen leaves. But it is distinguished by having yellow instead of red flowers. The two may hybridize, and flowers with characteristics of both are common in many areas. Still another mat-forming plant with urn-shaped flowers is *Cassiope mertensiana,* called white mountain heather or white moss heather. In this case the leaves are arranged in four tiers around the stem and pressed to it, forming overlapping scales. Look for all these species in the windy, open areas above timberline, associated with the Tolmie saxifrage and western pasque flower.

Range: Alaska south to Mt. Shasta along the high Cascades; also the Olympic Mountains and the northern Rockies.

White Mountain Heather

140

Mountain Heather

SPREADING PHLOX
Phlox diffusa
PHLOX Family

Forming dense carpets on the rocky slopes at and above timberline, this colorful plant has many characteristics typical of alpine flora; it grows low to the ground, thus avoiding the wind; has a deep root system to absorb water and store sugars; and it is perennial, the same plant surviving from one season to the next. It grows so slowly that it may spread just a few inches a year, blooming only after several growing seasons. Depending on elevation and exposure, spreading phlox may be found blooming during the entire summer. The cushions of short, green leaves may be covered by half-inch flowers, ranging in color from a rich blue to pale pink or white. The deep red color of some species of phlox resulted in the name, taken from the Greek word for flame. There are over 50 species of phlox native to North America and northern Asia.

Range: High mountains of the Northwest.

Spreading Phlox

COLLOMIA
Collomia debilis
PHLOX Family

A short-stemmed plant, collomia grows in dense mats, its leaves clustered together and its stems covered with tiny white hairs. The small, trumpet-shaped flowers are a pale purple or lavender. Although collomia may grow nearly one foot tall, it is usually only 2 or 3 inches high. A plant is usually in the shape of a low, rounded mound. This flower may be found on talus slopes and among volcanic rocks high above timberline, enjoying the company of few other plants. It may be found on the North and Middle Sister and on the high slopes of Mt. Hood, Mt. Jefferson and Lassen Peak. The genus name comes from the Greek word *kolla,* meaning glue, and refers to the sticky qualities of the moist seeds of some members of this genus.

Range: High peaks of the Cascades, northern Sierra Nevada, and the northern Rocky Mountains.

Collomia

TIMBERLINE PHACELIA
Phacelia hastata
WATER-LEAF Family

Tucked between the boulders of talus banks or growing flat against the gray granules of volcanic slopes above timberline, this phacelia is a compact plant, barely reaching 6 inches tall. The densely-clustered leaves are covered with flattened, stiff hairs that make the leaves bristly to the touch. The flowers are white or pale blue and are borne at the tip of the coiled stems. The stamens extend beyond the petals, giving the flowers a lacy appearance. This species of phacelia also grows at lower elevations; the plant treated here, found at higher elevations, is more properly called *Phacelia hastata* var. *compacta.*

Timberline phacelia is found only by those who venture above the level of trees and shrubs in the high Cascades. Since it is a low, prostrate plant, even then it is easy to overlook. It can be found above timberline on the volcanic peaks of the Cascades.

Range: Cascades of Washington and Oregon, south into the Sierra Nevada and east into Nevada.

Timberline Phacelia

DAVIDSON'S PENSTEMON
Penstemon davidsonii
FIGWORT Family

Also called creeping penstemon, beardtongue. Growing on open rocky slopes below and at timberline, this penstemon has small leathery, ovate leaves. A rock-hugging plant growing only about 6 inches tall, it adorns high alpine areas with its deep lavender-colored flowers. Although it is of short stature, this penstemon is sometimes considered to be a shrub because the stems rise from a distinctively woody base.

It is easily confused with Scouler's or shrubby penstemon *(P. fruticosus)*, which also has a woody stem and leathery leaves. Both grow in the rocky slopes and ledges above timberline. However, *Penstemon fruticosus* has narrow leaves, often with toothed edges, has blue or purple flowers, and is a little taller—up to 20 inches tall. It occurs from the foothills area to high elevations from southern British Columbia south through Oregon, mainly east of the Cascade crest.

Range: British Columbia south through the Cascades and Sierra Nevada; also Olympic Mountains.

Davidson's Penstemon

INDIAN PAINTBRUSH
Castilleja hispida
FIGWORT Family

Paintbrushes are very conspicuous segments of the alpine flora, generally occurring in bright red or scarlet colors. They may carpet entire meadows, both above and below timberline. For a discussion of a paintbrush more commonly found in lower elevation meadows, see page 116.

This paintbrush has bright scarlet bracts and its upper leaves have narrow lobes, often in threes. The entire plant is hairy—hispida means shaggy—and grows 6 to 18 inches tall. It is not confined to alpine areas and may also be found in lowland valleys.

A paintbrush that covers Paradise Valley on Mt. Rainier and is found in open meadows and woods near timberline throughout the Cascade Mountains is the rosy paint-brush *(Castilleja parviflora)*. A particularly brilliant plant, it is sometimes called magenta paintbrush because of the purplish color of its bracts. It grows 6 to 12 inches tall and its leaves have three to five deeply cut lobes. A yellow-bracted paintbrush, *Castilleja arachnoidea,* is common in the Three Sisters area, especially in Broken Top Crater, and in the lava flats of Mt. Shasta. It is a short plant, growing only about 6 inches tall. The soft, yellow tuft of bracts gives rise to its common name, cotton paintbrush.

Range: Cascade Mountains and northern Rocky Mountains.

Indian Paintbrush

Cotton Paintbrush

Rosy Paintbrush

HAREBELL
Campanula rotundifolia
HAREBELL Family

Also called bellflower, bluebell. Widely distributed throughout the northern portions of North America, these flowers are known in legend and folklore as "bluebells of Scotland." They may grow to 18 inches high, their slender stems having narrow, grass-like leaves. Younger plants, in addition have rounded, basal leaves that usually disappear by the time the flowers bloom. (It is this leaf that accounts for the species name rotundifolia, which means round leaf.) The purple or pale blue, bell-shaped flowers hang downward from the stems and appear in late June, July or August. In sheltered spots at high elevations, they may still be seen in September, when nearly all other flowers have faded and dried. This harebell may be found at nearly any elevation and nearly any type of situation: moist or dry slopes, valleys, meadows, or rocky outcrops.

Range: Circumpolar, extending south in the mountains of North America to Mexico.

ASTER FLEABANE
Erigeron peregrinus
COMPOSITE Family

The asters and fleabanes are difficult to distinguish from each other and individual species of each are also hard to identify, even for professional botanists. Generally speaking, fleabanes bloom in the spring and summer while asters flower in late summer and fall although this is sometimes no help during the short alpine summer where spring becomes summer in such a short period of time. Also, the ray flowers of the fleabanes are usually more numerous and narrower than those of the aster. The name fleabane comes from the old practice of hanging these flowers in a room to rid it of fleas. (Also see page 90.)

This fleabane has purple or pink ray flowers and yellow disk flowers borne atop a 1 to 2 foot tall stem. The largest leaves are at the bottom of the stem, and may be 8 inches long. The stem leaves are alternate, the upper ones quite a bit smaller than those at the base. This is a colorful plant and can be seen along the length of the Pacific Crest Trail, being especially abundant around Mt. Hood, in the meadow above Sunshine Shelter in the Willamette National Forest, around Crater Lake, and at Kings Creek Meadows on Lassen Peak.

Range: Widespread in the mountains of western North America.

Aster Fleabane

ALPINE ASTER
Aster alpigenus
COMPOSITE Family

Also called dwarf purple aster. Common above timberline and high montane meadows, this petite flower is easily recognized. Its narrow, deep green leaves are all basal, up to 4 or 7 inches long. The floral head has purple ray flowers with yellow center flowers and is borne at the tip of a 4 to 10 inch stalk. The floral stem curves upward and appears to be growing from one side of the cluster of leaves. Sometimes a plant will have more than one floral head per plant. It often grows in small colonies and thrives on slopes of loose gravel and pumice or tucked between rocks.

Another common aster growing around timberline, *Aster ledophyllus* (called Cascade aster) grows a bit taller— 1 or 2 feet. Leaves extend up the entire length of the stem, and the plants normally grow in clumps. In early July they are mere nubbins poking through the moist soil above timberline and in the openings between scattered clumps of subalpine fir and mountain hemlock but color these same areas with a bluish-purple hue by the end of that month. Each floral head may be 1 or 2 inches across, and more than one may occur on a single plant.

Both of these asters may be found in the open areas of high elevations throughout the Cascades.

Range: Mountains of the Pacific states and also the northern Rocky Mountains.

Cascade Aster

Alpine Aster

PUSSYTOES
Antennaria alpina
COMPOSITE Family

Also called alpine everlasting. Growing on short, 1 to 4 inch stems, this pussytoes is found nestled between rocks and boulders on slopes at and above timberline. Its tight ball of flowers is furry-feeling. If you cup the floral heads between your fingers and rub your thumb over them, you will feel the softness of a kitten's paw and understand the origin of one of its common names. (See page 89 for an explanation of the name everlasting.) This *Antennaria* blooms from mid-July through August and has paddle-shaped basal leaves and alternately arranged linear stem leaves. The stem and leaves are covered with tiny hairs, giving the whole plant a fuzzy appearance.

Range: Circumpolar, south at alpine elevations to California and Colorado.

SILVER RAILLARDELLA
Raillardella argentea
COMPOSITE Family

Growing in open pumice areas, silver raillardella is a small plant, a trait characteristic of high alpine species. The floral head is composed solely of yellow, tubular flowers, there being no ray flowers. A single floral head sits atop a 1 to 4 inch leafless stem—all the leaves are basal and are covered with silvery hairs. The plant is often found in small colonies so that a large area may be covered with these soft, silvery leaves, identifying the plants even when they are not in bloom. The flowers appear in July or August, depending on the elevation and location. Look for it in the Green Lakes area and Broken Top near the Three Sisters, the Watchman bordering Crater Lake, and near Crescent Crater in Lassen Volcanic National Park.

Range: Sierra Nevada and the southern Cascades.

Silver Raillardella

FALSE AGOSERIS
Nothocalais alpestris
COMPOSITE Family

A low, alpine plant about 4 to 12 inches high, false agoseris reminds one of the common dandelion. It has a single yellow floral head on each stem and a rosette of narrow, sometimes toothed or lobed basal leaves, each from 2 to 6 inches long. It grows on slopes and open meadows at higher elevations throughout the Cascades and may be found at McKenzie Pass, in Broken Top Crater, and in pumice areas around Crater Lake.

It could be confused with the orange agoseris, also called mountain dandelion *(Agoseris aurantiaca)*, which is superficially very similar and is closely related, but has an orange-red floral head instead of a yellow one. Like the *Nothocalais,* orange agoseris has a single floral head atop a slender stem and a rosette of basal leaves. It may be taller, however, growing up to 20 inches high. It can be found in open areas around the rim of Crater Lake and around Todd Lake in the Deschutes National Forest. It grows in open meadows and woodlands at moderate to high elevations in the Cascades, Sierra Nevada, and the Rocky Mountains.

Range: Cascade and Sierra Nevada Mountains.

GLOSSARY

Alternate—occurring singly, not opposite.

Annual—lasting only one year.

Basal—at the base; e.g., leaves at the base of a plant.

Bract—a small, modified leaf, usually at the base of a flower or cluster of flowers.

Cyme—a flat-topped flower cluster.

Decumbent—lying down; growing along the ground.

Desiccate—to dry up.

Disk flower—the center, tubular flowers of a composite; e.g., the yellow flowers in the center of a daisy.

Habitat—the area where a plant grows.

Head—a very close, compact cluster of flowers.

Lanceolate—lance-shaped; much longer than broad.

Leaflet—one of the parts of a compound leaf.

Opposite—occurring directly across from each other.

Ovate—shaped like an egg.

Parasite—living in or on another organism.

Perennial—lasting from one year to the next.

Petal—one of the floral parts, usually colored.

Petiole—the leaf stalk.

Pistil—the central seed-bearing organ of a flower.

Prostrate—growing flat on the ground.

Ray flower—the flat, elongate flowers of a composite; e.g., the white marginal flowers of a daisy or the yellow flowers of a dandelion.

Rootstock—an underground root-like stem.

Rosette—a collection of leaves arranged circularly around the base of a plant.

Saprophyte—a plant growing on dead organic matter.

Sepal—modified leaves of a flower below the petals, usually green.

Sessile—stemless.

Simple—one piece, as opposed to compound (in leaves).

Spathe—a large bract enclosing a flower cluster.

Spatulate—narrow at the base and wide at the tip.

Spur—sac-like or tubular projection.

Stamen—the floral organ bearing the pollen.

Taproot—a stout vertical root.

Whorled—three or more similar organs radiating from the same spot; e.g., whorled leaves.

TYPICAL FLOWER PATTERNS

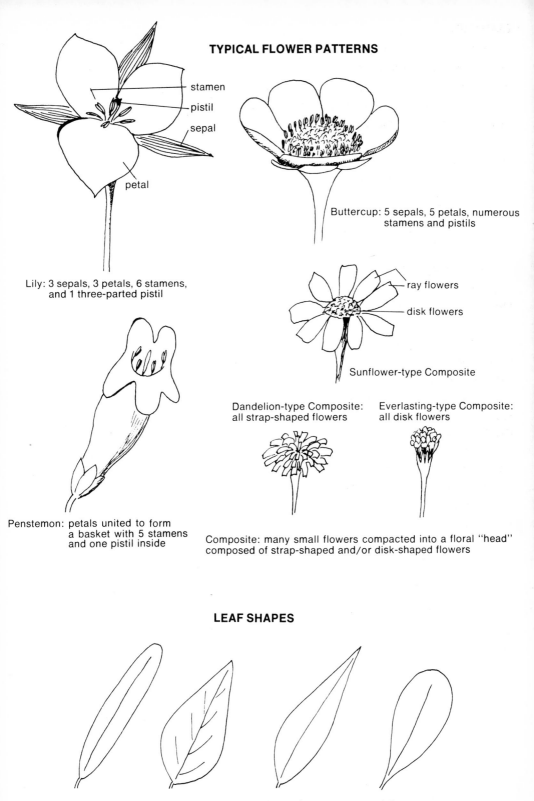

stamen
pistil
sepal
petal

Lily: 3 sepals, 3 petals, 6 stamens,
and 1 three-parted pistil

Buttercup: 5 sepals, 5 petals, numerous
stamens and pistils

ray flowers
disk flowers

Sunflower-type Composite

Dandelion-type Composite:
all strap-shaped flowers

Everlasting-type Composite:
all disk flowers

Penstemon: petals united to form
a basket with 5 stamens
and one pistil inside

Composite: many small flowers compacted into a floral "head"
composed of strap-shaped and/or disk-shaped flowers

LEAF SHAPES

linear   ovate   lanceolate   spatulate

LEAF ARRANGEMENTS

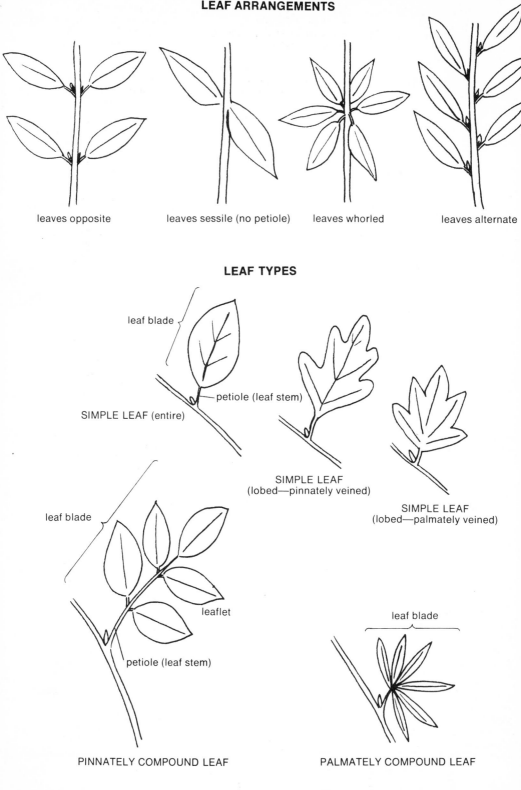

leaves opposite   leaves sessile (no petiole)   leaves whorled   leaves alternate

LEAF TYPES

leaf blade

petiole (leaf stem)

SIMPLE LEAF (entire)

SIMPLE LEAF
(lobed—pinnately veined)

SIMPLE LEAF
(lobed—palmately veined)

leaf blade

leaflet

petiole (leaf stem)

leaf blade

PINNATELY COMPOUND LEAF   PALMATELY COMPOUND LEAF

INDEX

Achillea millefolium, 86
Achlys triphylla, 34
Aconitum columbianum, 104
Actaea rubra, 32
Agoseris aurantiaca, 151
    false, 151
    orange, 151
Amelanchier alnifolia, 37
Anaphalis margaritacea, 84
Anemone deltoidea, 31
    lyallii, 31
    occidentalis, 131
    oregana, 31
Angel slipper, 27
Antennaria alpina, 149
    rosea, 89
Apocynum
    androsaemifolium, 77
Aquilegia flavescens, 102
    formosa, 102
Arctostaphylos
    columbiana, 76
    nevadensis, 76
    patula, 76
    uva-ursi, 76
Arenaria capillaris, 130
Arnica amplexicaulis, 87
    cordifolia, 87
    latifolia, 87
    longifolia, 87
    mollis, 87
Arnica, broad-leaf, 87
    clasping-leaved, 87
    hairy, 87
    heart-leaved, 87
    long-leaved, 87
Arrow-wood, 70
Arum Family, 94
Aruncus sylvester, 71
Asarum caudatum, 29
Asphodel, 97
Aster alpigenus, 148
    ledophyllus, 148
Aster, Alpine, 148
    Cascade, 148
    dwarf, 148
Azalea, Cascades, 75

Baneberry, 32
Barberry Family, 33-34
Beadlily, 21
Bearberry, 76
Beard tongue, 144
Beargrass, 58
Bellflower, 146
Berberis aquifolium, 33
    nervosa, 33
Bishop's cap, 36
Bird-bill, 111
Birthwort Family, 29
Bistort, American, 125
Bleedingheart Family, 61
Bluebells, 113, 146
Borage Family, 113

Bramble, dwarf, 39
Buckthorn Family, 73
Buckwheat Family, 125-128
Bugbane, false, 103
Bunchberry, 42
Buttercup Family, 31-32, 60,
    102-104, 131-133
Buttercup, subalpine, 133

Calochortus subalpinus, 124
    tolmiei, 124
Caltha biflora, 132
    leptosepala, 132
Calypso bulbosa, 27
Camas, common, 96
Camassia quamash, 96
Campanula rotundifolia, 146
Candyflower, 30
Cassiope mertensiana, 140
Castilleja arachnoidea, 145
    hispida, 145
    miniata, 116
    parviflora, 145
Cat's ear, 124
Ceanothus velutinus, 73
Chimaphila menziesii, 44
    umbellata, 44
Chinaberry, 32
Cinquefoil, fanleaf, 136
    Drummond's, 68
    shrubby, 136
    slender, 68
Claytonia lanceolata, 100
Clintonia uniflora, 21
Collomia debilis, 142
Coltsfoot, 119
Columbine, 102
Composite Family, 84-90,
    118-119, 147-151
Coolwort, 35
Corallorhiza maculata, 26
    mertensiana, 26
    striata, 26
Coral-root, 26
Cornus canadensis, 42
    nuttallii, 43
    stolonifera var.
    occidentalis, 110
Cow parsnip, 109
Cream-bush, 70
Currant, 63

Daisy, woolly yellow, 85
Dandelion, mountain, 151
Delphinium glareosum, 60
Desert parsley, few-
    fruited,139
Devil's club, 107
Dicentra formosa, 61
Dirty socks, 128
Dodecatheon alpinum, 111
    jeffreyi, 111
Dogbane Family, 77
Dogbane, spreading, 77

Dogtooth violet, 123
Dogwood Family, 42-43, 110
Dogwood, Pacific, 43
    red-osier, 110
Dwarf cornel, 42

Elephanthead, 115
Elderberry, blue, 82
    red, 82
Elkgrass, 58
Epilobium angustifolium, 74
Erigeron peregrinus, 147
    speciosus, 90
Eriogonum ovalifolium, 128
    pyrolaefolium, 128
    umbellatum, 128
Eriophyllum lanatum, 85
Erythronium grandiflorum, 123
    montanum, 123
Evening Primrose Family, 74
Everlasting, alpine, 149
    pearly, 84
    rosy, 89

Fairy slipper, 27
False bugbane, 103
Fernleaf, 115
Figwort Family, 53, 81,
    114-116, 144-145
Fireweed, 74
Fleabane, aster, 147
    large purple, 90
Foxfire, 79
Fragaria vesca, 65

Gaultheria, 50
Gentian Family, 112
Ghost pipe, 46
Gilia aggregata, 79
Gilia, skyrocket, 79
Ginseng Family, 107
Goat's beard, 71
Goldenrod, 118
Goodyera oblongifolia, 28
Grass-of-parnassus, 105
Groundsel, 87, 88

Habenaria dilatata, 98
    saccata, 98
Harebell Family, 146
Heath Family, 44-51, 75-76,
    140
Heather, 140
Hedgenettle, 80
Hellebore, 95
Heracleum lanatum, 109
Holodiscus discolor, 70
Honeysuckle, bush, 117
Honeysuckle Family, 54, 82,
    117
Huckleberry, black, 51
    fool's, 48
    rusty, 48
Hypopity's monotropa, 46

Indian pipe, 46
Inkberry, 117

Jacob's ladder, 78
Juneberry, 37
Johnny jump-up, 41

Kinnikinnick, 76
Knotweed, Newberry, 126

Ladies' tresses, 99
Larkspur, 60
Laurel, sticky, 73
Ligusticum grayi, 108
Lilium columbianum, 22
    washingtonianum, 59
Lily, avalanche, 123
    glacier, 123
    mariposa, 124
    sego, 124
    tiger, 22
    Washington, 59
Lily Family, 20-24, 58-59,
    95-97, 123-124
Linnaea borealis, 54
Listera caurina, 25
    cordata, 25
Lomatium martindalei, 139
Lonicera involucrata, 117
Lousewort, 53
Lovage, Gray's, 108
Luetkea pectinata, 137
Lungwort, tall, 113
Lupine, Anderson's, 72
    low mountain, 138
    subalpine, 72
Lupinus andersonii, 72
    latifolius, 72
    lepidus, 138
    lyallii, 138
Lysichitum americanum, 94

Maianthemum dilatata, 24
Manzanita, greenleaf, 76
    hairy, 76
    pinemat, 76
Marsh marigold, white, 132
Menziesia ferruginea, 48
Mertensia paniculata, 113
Mimulus guttatus, 114
    lewisii, 114
    moschatus, 114
    nanus, 114
    primuloides, 114
Mint Family, 80
Mitella breweri, 36
Mitrewort, 36
Moneses uniflora, 49
Monkeyflower, 114
Monkshood, 104
Monotropa uniflora, 46
    subalpine, 72
Montia sibirica, 30
Mountain ash, 64
Mountain misery, 75

Mountain pear, 37
Mountain sorrel, 127
Mountain spirea, 106
Mountain spray, 70

Nothocalais alpestris, 151
Nuphar polysepalum, 101

Ocean spray, 70
Oplopanax horridum, 107
Orchid, green bog, 98
    rattlesnake, 28
    white bog, 98
Orchid Family, 25-28, 98-99
Oregon grape, 33
Oxalis Family, 40
Oxalis oregana, 40
    trilliifolium, 40
Oxgria digyna, 127

Painted cup, 116
Paintbrush, common, 116
    cotton, 145
    Indian, 145
    magenta, 145
    rosy, 145
Parnassia fimbriata, 105
Parrotbeak, 53
Partridge foot, 137
Parsley, few-fruited
    desert, 139
Parsley Family, 108-109, 139
Pasque flower, 131
Pea Family, 72, 138
Pedicularis attolens, 115
    bracteosa, 115
    groenlandica, 115
    racemosa, 53
Penstemon, davidsonii, 144
    fruticosus, 144
    nemorosus, 81
    procerus, 81
    rupicola, 81
Penstemon, Davidson's, 144
    rock, 81
    Scouler's, 144
    shrubby, 144
    tall, 81
    woodland, 81
Petasites frigidus, 119
Phacelia hastata, 143
Phacelia, timberline, 143
Phlox diffusa, 141
Phlox Family, 78-79, 141-142
Phyllodoce empetriformis, 140
    glanduliflora, 140
Pinedrops, 45
Pinesap, 46
Pink Family, 130
Pipsissewa, 44
Polemonium californicum, 78
    pulcherrimum, 78
Polygonum bistortoides, 125
    newberryi, 126

Potentilla drummondii, 68
    flabellifolia, 136
    fruticosa, 136
    gracilis, 68
Primrose Family, 52, 111
Prince's pine, 44
Pterospora andromedea, 45
Purslane Family, 30, 100, 129
Pussypaws, umbellate, 129
Pussytoes, alpine, 149
    rosy, 89
Pyrola bracteata, 49
    picta, 49
    secunda, 49

Queen's cup, 21

Raillardella argentea, 150
Raillardella, silver, 150
Ranunculus eschscholtzii,
    133
Raspberry, trailing, 39
Rattlesnake orchid, 28
Rhododendron albiflorum, 75
    macrophyllum, 47
Rhododendron, Pacific, 47
    white, 75
Ribes howellii, 63
    sanguineum, 63
    viscosissimum, 63
Rosa gymnocarpa, 38
Rose Family, 37-39, 64-71,
    106, 136-137
Rubus lasiococcus, 39
    parviflorus, 66
    pedatus, 39
    spectabilis, 67

Salal, 50
Salmonberry, 67
Sambucus cerulea, 82
    racemosa, 82
Sandwort, 130
Saskatoon, 37
Saxifraga tolmiei, 135
Saxifrage Family, 35-36, 63,
    105, 135
Sedum divergens, 134
    oregonense, 62
Senecio integerrimus, 88
    triangularis, 88
Serviceberry, 37
Shadblow, 37
Shadbush, 37
Shinleaf, 49
Shooting star, alpine, 111
    Jeffrey, 111
Side-bells, 49
Single beauty, 49
Skunk cabbage, 94
Smilacina racemosa, 23
    stellata, 23
Snowbush, 73
Solidago canadensis, 118
Solomon's seal, 23

Sorbus sitchensis, 64
Sorrel, mountain, 127
    wood, 40
Spiraea betulifolia, 69
    densiflora, 106
    douglasii, 106
Spiranthes romanzoffiana, 99
Spirea, Alaska, 137
    birch-leaved, 69
    mountain, 106
    subalpine, 69
Spraguea umbellata, 129
Spring beauty, 100
Stachys cooleyae, 80
Starflower, 52
Steeplebush, 106
Stonecrop family, 62, 134
Strawberry, field, 65
Sulphur-flower, 128
Squawgrass, 58

Thimbleberry, 66
Tiarella trifoliata, 35
    unifoliata, 35
Tofieldia glutinosa, 97
Trautvetteria caroliniensis, 103

Trientalis arctica, 52
    latifolia, 52
Trillium ovatum, 20
Turtlehead, 81
Twayblade, 25
Twinberry, 117
Twinflower, 54

Vaccinium membranaceum 51
    ovalifolium, 51
Valerian, Sitka, 83
Valeriana sitchensis, 83
Vanilla-leaf, 34
Venus slipper, 27
Veratrum californicum, 95
    viride, 95
Viola adunca, 41
    glabella, 41
    macloskeyi, 41
    orbiculata, 41
Violet, dogtooth, 123
    Macloskey, 41
    Round-leaved, 41
    western long-
    spurred, 41
    wood, 41

Water-leaf family, 143
Water lily family, 101
White lilac, 73
Whortleberry, 51
Wild bleeding-heart, 61
Wild ginger, 29
Wild lily-of-the-valley, 24
Wild rose, 38
Windflower, 31
Wintergreen, 44
Wokas, 101
Wood betony, 115
Wood sorrel, 40
Wood trillium, 20
Wood violet, 41

Xerophyllum tenax, 58

Yarrow, 86
Yellow pond lily, 101

Zigadenus, 96

FOR FURTHER READING

Abrams, Leroy. *Illustrated Flora of the Pacific States.* Stanford: Stanford University Press, 1940, 1950, 1951, 1960. (4 volumes.)

Craighead, John J., Frank C. Craighead, Jr., and Ray J. Davis, *A Field Guide to Rocky Mountain Wildflowers.* Boston: Houghton Mifflin Company, 1963.

Dayton, William A. and others. *Range Plant Handbook.* Washington, D.C.: Government Printing Office. 1937.

Fernald, Merritt and Alfred C. Kinsey. *Edible Wild Plants of Eastern North America.* New York: Idlewild Press. 1943.

Gilkey, Helen M. and LaRea J. Dennis. *Handbook of Northwestern Plants.* Corvallis: Oregon State University Bookstores Inc., 1969.

Haskin, Leslie H. *Wildflowers of the Pacific Coast.* Portland: Binfords and Mort, 1959.

Hitchcock, C. Leo, Arthur Cronquist, Marion Ownbey and J. W. Thompson. *Vascular Plants of the Pacific Northwest.* Seattle: University of Washington Press, 1955, 1959, 1961, 1964, and 1969. (5 volumes.)

Lyons, C. P. *Trees, Shrubs, and Flowers to Know in Washington.* Vancouver: J. M. Dent and Sons, 1969.

Szczawinski and Hardy. *Guide to Common Edible Plants of British Columbia.* Victoria British Columbia Provincial Museum, Department of Recreation and Conservation. 1962.

FLOWER PHOTO TIPS

All of the photos in this book were made with a 35mm single lens reflex camera. The flowers were photographed in their natural setting, using available light. While there are advantages to moving a plant indoors to avoid wind and to control lighting, the natural setting tells more about the plant itself and hints at the type of place where the plant will be found. Your equipment need not be extensive—a good camera, a close-up lens or attachment, a light meter, and a tripod comprise the only essentials. But, alone, they will not produce a good picture.

Perhaps the single most important ingredient in photographing mountain wildflowers is patience—endless patience. As important as actually tripping the shutter is an awareness of the right situation. Good photos are created or made, not taken. Is there adequate lighting? Is the wind calm? Is the background clear of telephone wires, buildings, and road cuts? Is the flower a good specimen, not about to fade or half eaten by insects? Are you in a creative and objective mood and not in a hurry? If you can answer yes to all these questions, you are ready to photograph. Be willing to wait for or search out the best possible situations. The following are some suggestions that will help you make a good picture.

1. Get as close as possible to the flower. If one specimen is very small and you can not completely fill your frame, find several flowers growing together and photograph the group. Do not waste a portion of your picture unless the background really adds something to the finished photo.

2. When looking through your lens, look at the background and foreground as well as at the flower. Are there any sticks or leaves that will detract from your subject? (A piece of string or wire can be used to hold a branch up or away from the plant you are photographing. A small rock can hold down an intruding tuft of grass.) Sunlight bouncing off a shiny rock or smooth log in the background can cause a glare that will ruin an otherwise good picture. You may want to carry a piece of colored blotter paper (poster paper usually has a glossy surface and will reflect light; blotter paper will not) with you to place behind a flower to simplify a cluttered background. A large, dark-colored bathroom towel draped over branches or a bush can hide a confusing background.

3. Above timberline and in the sub-alpine meadows there is nearly always a faint breeze; more often it is a gusty, brisk wind. While it may be calmer in a dense forest of Douglas fir or mountain hemlock, there is still usually a faint whisper of wind. The slender stems of most plants sway slightly even when the air seems calm. With a wind, they dance wildly. When this is the case, you will be better to simply come back later. Unless there is a great deal of light so that you can use an extremely fast shutter speed, the flower will be a blur. Many people photograph early in the morning or late in the afternoon, when it is often calm. Others use a portable windbreak. A piece of clear plastic strung between two sticks is invisible to the camera, but will break the force of the wind. Sometimes a carefully placed knapsack can do the same thing. You may find yourself waiting 5 or 10 minutes to catch a flower between gusts of wind, but the wait will be worth it.

4. When photographing a white or bright yellow flower in the sunlight, take your light reading directly from the flower. The darker background will influence the meter and determine the reading, resulting in an overexposed flower.

5. Bright sunlight produces harsh shadows, which can be distracting at certain times. "Cloudy bright" light often produces rich colors and can be very favorable for flower photography.

6. Try carrying a small spray bottle with you to "freshen-up" your subject. Sometimes the leaves of plants, especially if near a dirt road, become coated with dust. Wash them off. A fine mist of water will give a dewy effect for your photo. (This can be overdone—you don't want *all* your pictures to look as if the flowers had dew on them!)

7. A shadowed background helps a meadow flower stand out. Have someone stand where his shadow falls behind the plant.

8. A reflector—white or light colored paper, aluminum foil, white shirt—can be used effectively to put light in areas of the picture where shadows are distracting.

It should take a great deal longer to "create" the picture you want than simply to "take" a picture. Do all you can to make a good photo before you trip the shutter. Your camera will do the rest.

E.L.H.